# UNLOCK GOD'S PURPOSE
# FOR YOUR
# RETIREMENT

A COLLABORATIVE RESOURCE BY IWORK4HIM

## JIM & MARTHA BRANGENBERG
## TED HAINS

HIGH BRIDGE BOOKS
HOUSTON

High Bridge Books titles may be purchased in bulk for educational, business, fundraising, or sales promotional use. For information, please contact High Bridge Books via www.HighBridgeBooks.com/contact.

Photograph by Gernelle Nelson Lifestyle Photography.

Published in Houston, Texas by High Bridge Books

# Growing Old God's Way

*O LORD, I have come to you for protection; don't let me
be disgraced.*

*Save me and rescue me, for you do what is right. Turn
your ear to listen to me, and set me free.*

*Be my rock of safety where I can always hide. Give the
order to save me, for you are my rock and my fortress.*

*My God, rescue me from the power of the wicked, from
the clutches of cruel oppressors.*

*O Lord, you alone are my hope. I've trusted you, O
LORD, from childhood.*

*Yes, you have been with me from birth; from my mother's
womb you have cared for me. No wonder I am always
praising you!*

*My life is an example to many, because you have been
my strength and protection.*

*That is why I can never stop praising you; I declare your
glory all day long.*

*And now, in my old age, don't set me aside. Don't aban-
don me when my strength is failing.*

*For my enemies are whispering against me. They are
plotting together to kill me.*

*They say, "God has abandoned him. Let's go and get him,
for no one will help him now."*

*O God, don't stay away. My God, please hurry to help
me.*

*Bring disgrace and destruction on my accusers. Humili-
ate and shame those who want to harm me.*

*But I will keep on hoping for your help; I will praise you more and more.*

*I will tell everyone about your righteousness. All day long I will proclaim your saving power, though I am not skilled with words.*

*I will praise your mighty deeds, O Sovereign LORD. I will tell everyone that you alone are just.*

*O God, you have taught me from my earliest childhood, and I constantly tell others about the wonderful things you do.*

*Now that I am old and gray, do not abandon me, O God. Let me proclaim your power to this new generation, your mighty miracles to all who come after me.*

*Your righteousness, O God, reaches to the highest heavens. You have done such wonderful things. Who can compare with you, O God?*

*You have allowed me to suffer much hardship, but you will restore me to life again and lift me up from the depths of the earth.*

*You will restore me to even greater honor and comfort me once again.*

*Then I will praise you with music on the harp, because you are faithful to your promises, O my God. I will sing praises to you with a lyre, O Holy One of Israel.*

*I will shout for joy and sing your praises, for you have ransomed me.*

*I will tell about your righteous deeds all day long, for everyone who tried to hurt me has been shamed and humiliated. (Psalm 71 NLT)*

# Dedication

This book is dedicated to the memory of the "old" version of thousands of retired Christ-followers. My friend and brother-in-law, Gary, was one of those floundering retired Christ-followers who had no idea what to do with his retirement. After spending years walking alongside our storyteller Ted Hains, Gary is on an impactful journey of living out his faith in his retirement. I hope and pray the same for you.

—**Jim Brangenberg**

# Contents

# Introduction

THERE IS A THREAD OF mentoring stitched through the many phases of my life. In seventh grade, my youth pastor invested time in my life and introduced me to the narrow path paved by Jesus. In high school, a college student mentored me for several years. In my early 20s, two business couples invested their lives into Martha and me, guiding us on the unique path of being an entrepreneurial couple. In my 30s, several pastors devoted time from their busy schedules to help keep me on the narrow road. And in my 40s, God blessed me with several mentors to reveal the significance of my work as a ministry. Today, I have three men that love the Lord and invest their time to help me to serve God the best way possible.

*It is powerful, it is personal, and it is purposeful.*

Mentoring changed my life and can change the trajectory of any life. It is powerful, it is personal, and it is purposeful. Jesus used it with His 12 disciples and the 72. Investing your life in that of another is the way to most closely mirror how Jesus spent His time on earth.

I am not retired. I don't know if I will ever officially be retired by the American definition, but living in Florida has allowed me to meet a lot of retirees. Most of my friends, neighbors, and fellow church members are retired. These friends have shared some of their life perspectives with me. They feel like they are off the field and have been placed in the grandstands of life. They feel relegated to watch the youngsters run the plays of life while they sit back and miss all the action.

*iRetire4Him: Unlock God's Purpose for Your Retirement* is a call to those in the grandstands to come back on the playing field of life, to mentor those running the plays. The opportunity to mentor the next generation is abundant and brings the personal purpose reminiscent of a job well done while allowing the flow of unrestricted faith. *iRetire4Him: Unlock God's Purpose for Your Retirement* is dedicated to helping you find faith-centered purpose in your retirement as you live out the best days of your life. Powerful, personal purpose can be found by investing your life into the life of another, in the form of mentoring.

Ted Hains adds impactful stories to the end of each chapter, and you will also meet some great ministries that embrace retirees. Join us on an incredible journey of preparing to live with purpose, investing in others, and joyfully declaring iRetire4Him. I am asking you to spend your retirement years mentoring the next generations. You may be the parental figure referred to in this scripture.

> My son, obey your father's godly instruction and follow your mother's life-giving teaching. Fill your heart with their advice and let your life be shaped by what they've taught you. Their wisdom will guide you wherever you go and keep you from bringing harm to yourself. Their instruction will whisper to you at every

sunrise and direct you through a brand-new day. (Prov. 6:20–22 TPT)

—**Jim Brangenberg**, iWork4Him

## Ted Hains, Author and Storyteller

Every chapter of *iRetire4Him* ends with a true story from the life of my (Martha's) dad, Ted Hains. Ted spent his career as a portrait photographer and recalls feeling much like Moses with a staff in hand, asking God to use the camera that he was carrying to fulfill God's plan for his life. He's passionate about using his gifts and talents for the Lord during retirement.

Ted is currently serving as a board member of iWork4Him Ministries, Inc. and Ambassador for iRe-

tire4Him. He enthusiastically helps his peers learn to live the "iRetire4Him" lifestyle. Ted uses his newest hobby, woodturning, as an open door to conversations that lead to his faith. He is also a member of the Pocket Testament League, where he speaks on their behalf and passes out John's Gospel daily.

He and his wife of 64 years, Elaine, split their time between Cass Lake, Minnesota, and Fort Myers, Florida.

They have three daughters and one son, eight grandchildren, and fourteen great-grandchildren scattered across the United States.

Always able to share an application, Ted has generously poured out his memories for our benefit. Ted lives with faith at the center. His professional career had many peaks and valleys by the world's standards, but he has chosen growth through adversity and success. Enjoy the look behind the curtain as Ted shares his life lessons from the heart. I am blessed to be his daughter and have had a front-row seat to this life well lived.

*Thanks, Dad, for being such a great example to me, our family, your employees, friends, and the people who will read this book. You and mom have lived and worked through the filter of the Gospel, and I am eternally grateful. I love you.*

*—Your daughter, Martha*

*I am grateful for your daughter and you, Ted. She is an amazing gift from God that you and Elaine stewarded so well.*

*—Thank you, Jim*

## Before We Begin...

Most of the narratives in this book come from me, Jim Brangenberg, except where otherwise noted. When I refer to "us," I mean my wife, Martha, and me.

# Part I

THE FOLLOWING PAGES CALL you to put your faith into action in your retirement years. We desire to lead Christ-following retirees to declare iRetire4Him openly. On the iWork4Him show, we have interviewed over 3,000 people who are living out their faith in their work. While these people connected their faith at work, many weren't sure how living out their faith in their retirement would look. We realized that Christians are looking for the same kind of clarity for living out their faith in their retirement years. We recognized the need for a written resource to encourage you, the everyday retired believer, to live out your faith with intentionality in your retirement years.

Part I of *iRetire4Him* brings you the practical, tactical, factual, and biblical ways of putting your faith into action in the retirement phase of life.

We hope you walk away challenged and equipped to impact your retirement mission field.

# 1

---

# Retirement Redefined

---

*iRetire4Him*: It's a statement about life, a declaration of faith, and a life plan. It is also a challenge worth choosing. iRetire4Him ignites the journey to redefining retirement. Let's break it down.

i

Me, myself, and i. The lower case i makes someone else the focus. He is. It is a personal statement that declares a conviction.

## Retire

Retirement is a concept brought on by the postindustrial man in the 1950s. Before 1980, most people never lived much past 65 or 70 because they worked so hard. Americans equate retirement from a job to retiring from life. By definition, retirement means to pull away or withdraw. Financial retirement leads many to stop their career and withdraw from purpose and productivity.

The Bible only has one mention of retirement. At age 50, the Levitical priest stepped out of the priesthood's physical phase and into a mentoring phase. Butchering animals for sacrifice in the temple was hard work and involved a lifetime of learning. This single example of retirement in scripture is a great model for the modern retiree.

> *We ask God to give you complete knowledge of His will and to give you spiritual wisdom and understanding.*
> —*Colossians 1:9 NLT*

Instead of sitting in the grandstands watching the younger generations lead the Kingdom on earth, retirement can be a chance to get back on the playing field, mentoring and coaching the action in your area of expertise.

## 4

3 + 1 = 4. The Father, Son, and Holy Spirit + You. Add yourself into the equation with the Trinity of God. Work together with the Heavenly Father in your life. He teaches us to focus on others. Not for you but 4 Him to be 4 others.

## Him: Almighty God

Him with a capital H is our Heavenly Father. When we focus on Him in this last phase of life, He is in the spotlight of all we do. Jeremiah 29:11 tells us that He knows the plans for our future. Let's do it for Him.

Most of us work with our eyes set on some version of the American Dream: a second home, winters in the south, endless rounds of golf, sleeping in, no calendar, no boss, etc. This list sounds good. But is that all retirement offers? Will this list lead to peace and contentment or leave you bored and resentful? iRetire4Him means you can enjoy some of these things and still have a purpose that makes you want to get up in the morning.

The American Dream of retirement has deceived many of us. The American Dream promises wealth and prosperity with a lifetime of vacation, but it's filled with empty promises and false hopes. The American Dream doesn't lead to peace and contentment. It leads to boredom and poor health. We all know someone searching for a purpose in life. They won't find it in constant pleasure. Most of them would give anything to be back at work, even the work they were doing for the last 40 years. Work appeared to provide them with purpose.

*To talk about retirement, we need to learn about work.*

To talk about retirement, we need to learn about work. Work was provided by God to bring glory to Him. Our Father in Heaven is a worker, and we are to be like Him throughout our lives.

In Genesis 1 and 2, God laid out His plan for mankind. His blueprint included many responsibilities, but essentially, He directed us to work. He also commanded a day of rest every week to refresh and focus on family and Him. It is very important to recognize that work was given to Adam and Eve as a gift. It was not a result of the curse of sin. We know that work is a gift because we love to work. Maybe you didn't love the work you had been doing, but you love it when you work and receive a sense of accomplishment. Re-read Genesis 2 and see how God created work for us. It was good.

As I mentioned before, retirement is only mentioned once in the Bible. Numbers 8:23–26 instructs the Levites to work from the age of 25 to 50. Even after the age of 50, they are encouraged to support the priest but no longer officiate in the service.

The Bible doesn't teach an end to our working years. Instead of saying, "I retired," you can learn to say "iRetire4Him." In this phase, we can have purpose and direction without the demands of the daily grind. Consider serving those in the game rather than sitting in the bleachers as spectators.

> Don't copy the behavior and customs of this world, but let God transform you into a new person by changing the way you think.
> (Rom. 12:2 NLT)

This verse is crucial to understand. As Jesus followers, we get to live a transformed life different from the world around us. For us to do that, we need to change the way we think. Retirement, the way the world touts it, is different than God's desire for your life. He wants you part of the game, not sitting in the stands. God made you in His image. He is a worker, and so are you. So, let's embrace iRetire4Him and see what's next.

## Ted Hains Shares a Story: Sin Comes Naturally

My brother, sister, and I often email pictures back and forth from our childhood. This morning, my sister Joyce sent us a photograph of three children (not related to us) and said that the beautiful little girl holding a darling baby could have been her as a child holding her baby brother. The older boy in the picture was holding the baby's nose while innocently looking away. My brother and I are known for that kind of behavior.

She referenced a childhood story of how I stuffed an electrical plug down her throat at age two and a half. She says that's exactly the way mom told it to her. My dad told me it was just one of those grey metal knockout things the size of a nickel from an electrical box.

Either way, it would appear my intent was not good. The original sin was now fully engaged in that little boy in the photo, and Joyce saw the similarity between him and me.

Once, when Joyce was a toddler and I was five years old, I became her hero. Back in the 1930s, it was not unusual for people to have goldfish ponds in their backyards with no fence or screening of any kind. One summer day, my sister wandered right into the neighbor's pond. Enter the five-year-old superhero, Teddy. I rescued her as all the neighbors rejoiced. Joyce, the two-year-old toddler, remembers clearly that I pushed her in. That's her story, and she's sticking to it. All of this transferred back and forth by text this morning. Roger, my much younger brother, said in a text to me: *"I think the real message here is the spiritual growth past our original sin."* I cut and pasted the words right here from his message, so it's 100% genuine. I think he's trying to tell us that a lot of growth has happened since then, and there seems to be a lot of sins in our lives for which we need forgiveness.

Bottom Line: We don't need to go to school to learn how to sin. It just comes naturally, whether you are three, 33, or 83. In our work or our retirement, we often get caught up in focusing on other people's sin issues. Today, look at your own sin issues and work on them. God is the ultimate healer, and He loves to help us move from a sinful life to an obedient life.

## Chapter 1 Questions

1. How many years have you dreamed about retiring?

2. Had you considered that God has an intentional plan for your retirement years?

3. Ted talks about sin issues plaguing him as a kid and even as an 88-year-old retiree. What sin issues are you currently working through or need to focus on today?

# 2

## iRetire4Him: Changing

*Is not wisdom found among the aged? Does not long
life bring understanding?*

—Job 12:12 NIV

YOUR LONG LIFE IS A blessing. Your wisdom can make a difference. When we stand before the Lord, and He asks us
about our time on earth, He isn't just asking about our
time before we retire. He wants to say about our whole
lives: "Well done, good and faithful servant."

I thought peer pressure would go away after high
school, but it still seems to linger into retirement. You've
seen the choices of greeting cards for retirement: the land-
scape usually includes a glass of iced tea and either the
beach, mountains, or golf course on the horizon. The as-
sumption is that retirees are comfortable financially and
mentally, have their health, have many friends, and everybody is chilling out all day long, every day. I remember
my mom saying to me, "Just because everyone is doing it
doesn't mean you have to. I mean, really, if all your
friends were jumping off a bridge, does that mean you

have to jump off the bridge, too?" Just because everyone is doing it doesn't make it right, even in retirement.

Romans 12:2 is counter-cultural and revolutionary. It is a revelation about how God views our lives as Christ-followers. In the NLT version, it reads:

> Don't copy the behavior and customs of this world, but let God transform you into a new person by changing the way you think. Then you will learn to know God's will for you which, is good and pleasing and perfect.

If you and I are busy copying the world's behaviors and customs, we will miss what God has for us. He has a better way. Isaiah said it best.

> "For my thoughts are not your thoughts, neither are your ways my ways," declares the LORD. "As the heavens are higher than the earth, so are my ways higher than your ways and my thoughts than your thoughts." (Isa. 55:8–9 NIV)

What does it look like to retire from a biblical perspective instead of a worldly perspective? When you embrace the iRetire4Him lifestyle, you embrace the Lord's plan for your life. iRetire4Him will look different for each of us because of where we live and what life skills we have to share.

If you are a Christ-follower,

*iRetire4Him will look different for each of us because of where we live and what life skills we have to share.*

here is a list of things your retirement years won't look like:

- Being on vacation every day with no cares in the world
- Playing all the time
- Watching TV all day long
- Reading books all the time

It's not inappropriate doing some of these things some of the time. However, as retired Christ-followers, we need to be involved in our local society at a much higher level. When we retire, we have more time to be intentional with our days. Here are some key questions to ask yourself as you look for God's plan in your retirement:

- What do I love to do?
- Who are the people in my life that I can serve?
- With the skills that I have, who should I invest my time in?
- With my unique position in my local community, how can I serve it with the example of Christ's love?
- While on my vacations/golf outings/dinner gatherings, how can I intentionally interject my faith in Jesus into the conversations?
- How can I encourage my kids and their peers in their faith?

- How can I encourage my grandkids and their peers in their faith?

- How can I use the wisdom that God has given me to shape the life of another?

Ask the Lord to prepare you for this next phase of life right now. Get out of the grandstands of life and get back into the game. You will be going against the grain, so when you start to look at your life through the lens of iRetire4Him, your friends may think you are crazy. That's okay. When you go all-in for Jesus, your life is going to look different than other folks.

I encourage you to surround yourself with other Christ-followers who are tired of an empty life of retirement. You can hold each other accountable for changing the way you think.

## Ted Hains Shares a Story: The Ring

In 1955, I drove my girlfriend, Elaine, from Rock Island, Illinois, to her hometown in Michigan for what turned out to be the worst Christmas of our lives. She was a senior in nurse training, and I was busy setting up my new photo studio. After Christmas Eve service, we opened gifts with her parents, and I surprised her with a package containing an engagement ring. She truly had no idea about the gift until she saw it taped to a lovely heart-shaped compact. Her parents hardly spoke a word about it during the drive to spend Christmas Day with a relative. When we arrived, her mom said she wouldn't get out of the car until Elaine gave me back the ring. Reluctantly, I put it in my pocket, and we went about the day as if nothing had happened. It was a very sad day for us. It was quiet driving home to Rock Island. But in a few days, it would be a New Year with new starts. The bottom line was they were angry with me for not properly asking her father for permission to marry his daughter, and they felt I was not a good enough person to marry Elaine. We continued dating and knew we were meant for each other. On her 21st birthday, May 16, 1956, Elaine proudly wore the diamond ring as a symbol of our intent.

Next, we consulted with my Pastor and the Hospital Chaplain, where Elaine was in nurse training. They were both convinced that our love was strong and felt that we would make a good match. With that information, Elaine called her parents and asked them if she could come home and be married in her childhood Lutheran church. Her mother asked if she was pregnant. Elaine said, "no." That was her mother's answer, too. *No*, she couldn't come home for a wedding. No amount of tears and pleading would soften her mother's heart and give us her parents' permission. This conversation with her mom was a real blow to her vision of what a wedding day could be.

We wrestled with questions like "How can a mother and father reject their child like that? Doesn't the Bible say we are to leave our mother and father and cleave to our spouse?" It was especially hard to understand the rejection of her dad. Elaine had always been his buddy, the one he took fishing and to his gas station to hang out.

Elaine's parents did come to Rock Island in August for her graduation, but very little was said. My parents tried to befriend them, but that didn't go well. They were upset with Elaine for not returning to Michigan after graduation.

An outstanding orthopedic doctor in Moline, Illinois, hired Elaine as his scrub nurse. She and several classmates rented the upstairs of a home in the same town. With these details in place, we set the wedding date as Oct. 7, 1956. My buddy Delbert agreed to be my best man, and his wife Sally loaned Elaine her wedding gown. Elaine asked her sister if she could borrow her wedding dress, but she refused to lend it, fearing her mother's retaliation. We were married without the joy of any of her family attending.

Over the years, Elaine and I would travel to Michigan every Christmas and summer vacation so our children would always know their grandparents. The visits were extremely hard for me, as her mother and I usually ended up arguing about religion and the Bible. These conversations intensified as our spiritual journey took us to the Evangelical Free Church. The arguments further increased as we followed Christ in believers' baptism by emersion. "We had you baptized as an infant," they reminded her.

I realized I could not hate a person I was praying for, so I started praying for her mother daily, and my heart softened towards her.

Many years later, Elaine's mother had just turned 80. That Thanksgiving, Elaine said to me, "I would like to go alone to visit my mother to see if we can make our peace. You can have that time with your family." The time had come for reminiscing. As Elaine was attempting to tell her mom why she was coming, her mother said, "You know,

Elaine, you never did what you were capable of." In her late 50s, Elaine became a scolded child one more time. It was not long after that when Elaine's mom was on the phone with her sister Helen, and during their conversation, she had a heart attack. By the time Helen arrived at her mother's apartment, she was dead.

It was mid-winter when the funeral took place. The drive from our home in Minneapolis, Minnesota, to Grand Rapids, Michigan, was treacherous. Heavy snow and ice would typically have turned all of us around, but we pressed on. In a private conversation, I was asked how I felt about Elaine's mother suddenly passing. I said, "She can't hurt us anymore!" I decided always to choose to love who my children love.

Luke 6:28 says, "Bless those who curse you, pray for those who mistreat you" (NIV).

I struggle with Matthew 19:5 as well: "For this cause shall a man leave father and mother, and shall cleave to his wife" (KJV). Also, Exodus 20:12 says, "Honor your father and your mother, that your days may be long upon the land which the LORD your God is giving you" (NKJV). This year we celebrate our 64th anniversary. I guess God honors the cleaving.

Elaine has been editing these stories, and this one was particularly difficult for her. The old wounds resurfaced, and her heart ached once again with the memory of the pain surrounding our wedding. I admire her for the way she has sought the healing that can only come from God and the love He pours out to all who call upon Him.

Here's a life lesson: perhaps there is a ring in your life. Are you carrying an old wound or pain from the past? Seek out a trusted Christian that can guide you through the healing process of forgiveness. The weight of your burden can become light as you allow God's love to wash over you and soothe your broken heart. May God comfort you in this journey.

Bottom Line: Our words have power. Many of us have experienced family pain, similar to what I've described above. Elaine and I could have wallowed in this pain for the last 64 years of marriage, but we chose instead to forgive. I know this is a tough story to read, but as retired folks, we often forget about our words' power and the power of our approval. Please use this story as a reminder to mend bridges that are broken with family members, especially your children. Offer forgiveness where needed and ask forgiveness of those you have hurt. Your ministry in the iRetire4Him community is significant, but it pales compared to a healed relationship with your family. Our first ministry is to our family. If there is healing to do, lead the way.

## Chapter 2 Questions

1. What would it take to be counter-cultural in your retirement?

2. What would it look like to live with intentionality in your retirement years?

3. What is your ring? What tangible reminder could you have to remind you to speak words that heal, restore, connect, and build others up?

4. Ted shared some family problems and pain. What relationship can you mend before the Lord calls an end to your days?

# 3

## iRetire4Him: Covenant and Commitment

BARNA RESEARCH SAYS THAT 36% of the United States population identifies as born-again Christians. If we translate that percentage to retirees, that would mean there are at least 30 million Christian retirees. We have met a lot of retirees because we live in Florida. After the retiree honeymoon is over, many express that they become bored and don't feel that they have a purpose. They often live far away from kids and grandkids and want their days to matter, but don't know how to build in the intentionality they need for fulfillment. So far, retirement is leaving them empty. The iRetire4Him Covenant is here to jumpstart your new outlook as a retiree. You can commit to impacting future generations with the love of Jesus, one relationship at a time. To learn more and join the movement, please visit www.iwork4him.com/retire4him/join! While there, you can download the covenant and commitment you will find on the following pages.

# The iRetire4Him Covenant

My retirement has created the freedom to explore new ministry opportunities. My retirement ministry manual

is my Bible. My calling in retirement is not a second-class calling. I dedicate my retirement to God, and because of Jesus in my life, I am committed to celebrating whatever He brings my way.

## I COMMIT MYSELF TO:

## PRAYER:

**Pray for those I regularly meet by name each day.** Pay attention to people I interact with regularly, write down their names, and pray for them by name. 1 Timothy 2:1-5 (NLT) [1] I urge you, first of all, to pray for all people. Ask God to help them; intercede on their behalf, and give thanks for them.

## CARE:

**Find a way to serve those I pray for in a way that starts a relationship.** Look for ways to serve them through teaching life skills or job skills while living life together. Galatians 5:13-14 (NLT) [13] For you have been called to live in freedom... use your freedom to serve one another in love. [14] For the whole law can be summed up in this one command: "Love your neighbor as yourself."

**Invest time in these relationships so they will trust me when I share the truth.** Look for ways to befriend those I have written down. Find ways to get to know them and their family. Look for things to pray for them. Ecclesiastes 4:9-10 (NLT) [9] Two people are better off than one, for they can help each other succeed. [10] If one person falls, the other can reach out and help. But someone who falls alone is in real trouble.

## SHARE:

**Look for opportunities to pray with people when you notice they are having a tough day.** Look for ways to pray with them in the neighborhood, at church, or wherever we connect. Ask them how they are doing and then listen while they share. Matthew 18:20 (NLT) [20] For where two or three gather together as my followers, I am there among them."

**Be ready to share the hope that is in me, Jesus.** 1 Peter 3:15 (NLT) [15] Instead, you must worship Christ as Lord of your life. And if someone asks about your hope as a believer, always be ready to explain it.

## WORK:

**All along, be a person who represents excellence in everything I do.** Let your life be an example worth following through the excellence displayed in attitude and actions – showing them love and a desire for a relationship with them. Colossians 3:23 (NLT) [23] Work willingly at whatever you do, as though you were working for the Lord rather than for people.

# The iRetire4Him Commitment

## Who I am:

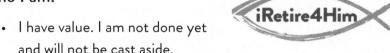

- I have value. I am not done yet and will not be cast aside.
- I have wisdom to transfer to the younger generations.
- I have a unique set of Spiritual Gifts, Talents, and Abilities
- I can volunteer or work and bless others with my skills and experiences.
- I can be a parent to the parentless or a grandparent to the grandparent-less.

## I see:

- That my country, church, and the next generation(s) need me.
- That I have value in God's eyes, and He is not done with me yet.

## I commit:

- To live intentionally in my neighborhood using tools like www.blesseveryhome.com.
- To seek out a younger man or woman to mentor or disciple.
- To run the race to the very end, recognizing that God wants to use my remaining years regardless of health or limitations.
- To fill my time with purpose and intentionality, to "work" in my city where I am needed most and seek to go where younger people are.

- To encourage my peers to get out of the grandstands and back onto the playing field.
- To challenge my church to find a way to integrate all generations, vs. separating them into "seasons of life" (to do life together, enable wisdom to transfer back and forth from old to young and young to old, and all ages and stages in between).
- To use my Spiritual Gifting and actively find ways to be useful for God and others.

## I will pray for:

- Opportunities to encourage Christians in their work.
- The clarity in where to use the wisdom, knowledge, and experience I gained during my work and life.
- A deeper relationship with God, which is all that I can take with me to Heaven.

I understand that retirement is only shifting from one phase of life to the next. I am needed and will respond to the call on my life. I commit to *Retire4Him*.


Signature: _____ Date: ___/___/___

## Ted Hains Shares a Story: Ralph

In the mid-1980s, a store in Minneapolis called Donaldson's went out of business. They were selling off all the store fixtures. So, I looked to see if I could find any treasures. I was drawn to a mannequin in a sitting position, bought him, and named him "Ralph."

I put my mannequin in the front seat of my minivan and buckled him in. I drove home with him, pulled up to the front of our photography studio, and parked the van. I went inside and told my wife that someone in the vehicle wanted to see her. Elaine went to the van, and upon seeing "Ralph," she jumped back, startled. Ralph had that effect on almost everybody that met him.

Once at a family gathering, Ralph came along, and we put him in the Lazy Boy recliner in the living room. Our granddaughter, Sarah, who must have been about three, came in the door, looked at Ralph, and started to cry. She wouldn't budge or come any further into the living room.

Elaine and I were going on vacation, and we asked our part-time employee Suzie to cover for us at the studio while we were gone. I put Ralph on the countertop in the darkroom and put a sign on the door saying, "Do not enter. Ralph's in here!" Suzie could not resist. A few days into our vacation, Suzie went into the darkroom, and upon seeing Ralph, she screamed and fell to her knees.

Ralph just had a way with women. Over the years, Ralph showed up at many family functions and became part of the family fun.

Ralph's final appearance was at grandson Joshua's high school graduation party, where Ralph was sitting on a lawn chair on the yacht that his parents had rented for the party. Ralph could no longer hold it together and started falling apart. His parts began showing up at other family gatherings. For instance, our grandson Tanner acquired his head, and it made the rounds to wedding anniversaries, birthdays, and other functions. There are many stories about Ralph, but just one thing was never talked about, authenticity. Ralph was merely a representation of the real thing. There will be no retirement for Ralph. He merely came apart and lost his head.

There must be a better end to our story than merely losing our head. Are we willing to focus our hearts on what God has called us to do? What is that for you? The Bible says to go to Jerusalem, Judea, Samaria, and the ends of the earth to spread the good news and teach others what Jesus taught the disciples. My Samaria is Fort Myers, Florida. What's yours?

Bottom Line: If we don't have a plan and a purpose focused on the calling God has for us in our retirement, we may lose our heads like Ralph. God has a plan for you until your last day. Do you know what it is?

## Chapter 3 Questions

1. What is your plan for engaging your neighbors in a relationship?

2. Are you willing to take the challenge to Retire4Him? If yes, go to www.iwork4him.com/retire4him/join and join the iRetire4Him Nation.

3. Ted introduces us to Ralph in this chapter's story. Ralph looked good and had a great tan. He was well sculpted and was the life of the party. But Ralph was fake and didn't have any life purpose except to look good. What is your plan for living out your retirement years with purpose, so you don't lose your head like Ralph?

# 4

# iRetire4Him: Mentor

YOUR RETIREMENT YEARS CAN have purpose through investing yourself in others with all that you know. We call that process mentoring, and you are the mentor. All the years you spent working and gaining valuable experience will not go to waste in your retirement. Through you, that experience is available to the next generation.

Large corporations often eliminate highly-paid experienced workers to save money. They don't consider the wisdom and knowledge gap created by removing the veterans from their team. How can we avoid the same mistake? Don't take yourself out of the game. Someone needs you today as a mentor in their life. You were looking for a purpose in retirement. It starts with becoming a mentor, and the world needs you to move forward on this idea right now.

New ideas can be exciting and overwhelming. When you think of building intentionality in your retirement years through mentoring, it can seem daunting. Let's look at being a mentor through the KISS (keep it simple, silly) principle. You don't have to go back to school or learn a particular program. Being a mentor is as simple as loving God and loving people. Jesus used the KISS principle to summarize the law and the prophets in two sentences. We know that Jesus understands complexity because He created the world, as well as calculus, physics, and time. Yet, Jesus used simplicity to confound the learned. We have all of the Old Testament laws and rules, yet he summed it up in two sentences. Love God. Love people. It can be your new mission statement. Love God. Love people.

> The man answered, "'You must love the LORD your God with all your heart, all your soul, all your strength, and all your mind.' And, 'Love your neighbor as yourself.'" (Luke 10:27 NLT)

If you love God, you will obey Him. If you love people, you will treat them well. It's that simple. Mentoring is about building relationships and sharing life. Our life lessons, and our faith in Jesus, can impact others through mentoring.

We will go into more detailed explanations of what mentoring looks like in the next chapter. For now, mentoring the next generations can look like this:

1. Teach the next generations in your life/church/neighborhood/family how to cook. Lots of talking happens when you cook, and young people appreciate good cooking just like anyone else. Make a meal together and sit around the table to enjoy it.

2. Invite the next generation for a car cleaning day. Washing, waxing, and general upkeep of a car happens shoulder-to-shoulder. Show

your mentee how to be a good steward of
their auto investment.

3. Hang out. Many of us live next door to
   younger people who have no family around,
   whether it's due to miles, alienation, being
   orphaned, or by choice. Your neighbor may
   be craving interaction with someone older
   and wiser.

What makes you a great mentor? Everything you have
learned in your life, the good and the bad, makes you a
great mentor. From God, you have a unique set of gifts,
talents, and abilities. That makes you a great mentor too.
How did you learn your work
skills? Are you good at it? Can
you use your skills to train
others? Are you willing?

*Everything you have
learned in your life,
the good and the
bad, makes you a
great mentor.*

Often, we learn our jobs
and then settle into a comfortable routine. Retirement can
be like that, too. We are relaxed, and training someone
to do a task or skill will take time and effort. Remember
when you were a rookie at your job? Remember how
grateful you were that someone took the time to teach you
your skill. My dad taught me how to shovel a driveway
and use a snowblower. Those skills made me a lot of money, which paid for my college education. Most of my
friends just sat inside and drank hot chocolate when I was
raking in cash. What kinds of things can you teach others?

Is teaching and mentoring a hassle or an opportunity? Mentoring allows you to share your life, skills, and experience, including the impact Jesus has had on you.

Parenting is much like this, as well. Mom and dad invest time, energy, and a lot of teaching in their children. They teach them about money, school, cars, and other stuff while showing them love, discipline, acceptance, direction, and wisdom. However, not everyone grows up in a household like this. That is where you fit in as a mentor. You can teach your mentee the ropes of life, show them excellence in work, and feed into them biblical truth.

Mentoring is a powerful way to pass on your God-given gifts to young people around you, but it doesn't have to be formal. Most of the real lessons I learned in life were not on the chalkboard or in the training manual. Most of the life lessons I learned came from people who invested their time in me, like a life apprenticeship class. For example, Mr. Conrad, my high school computer teacher, hired me to dig footings and foundations for the porches and decks he was building during the summer. I loved making $5.00 an hour, and I loved learning new things. Mr. Conrad mentored me for many summers. One summer, he said, "Jim, you will be a great programmer one day because you love to solve problems. You should get an IT degree." Because of Mr. Conrad's relationship with me and because the world in the early '80s was getting computerized, I got an IT degree. However, my father was right. He said I was a natural salesperson. I ended up selling computers, not programming them. I couldn't sit still long enough to do the programming. But the point is, Mr. Conrad had a powerful influence on my life, and I listened to his counsel and appreciated him very much. I do love to solve problems. I don't particularly enjoy doing the solving on a screen.

Stop. Look around. Who do you see? Do you know someone in the younger generation who can use a mentor in their life? Go slowly. Pray. Serve. Befriend. Let the Lord lead you intentionally into a relationship with a younger person. Guide them in life and to eternal life. You have it in you.

## Ted Hains Shares a Story: Retirement Isn't Biblical

Seventy-five years ago, I was in confirmation class with my pastor, William E. Berg, a wonderful man of God. He spent his life writing books, preaching, and sharing Jesus Christ. We stayed in touch over the years, and one of the last books he wrote was titled *A strange Thing Happened to Me on the Way to Retirement – I Never Arrived!* About a week before his death at the age of 103, he was still writing. Scripture reminds us that the only persons spoken of in the Bible allowed to retire were the Levitical priests. However, it never said that they couldn't have another vocation after retirement.

When I was born in 1932, the insurance actuaries had my life expectancy at 57. Consequently, I would never live long enough to receive social security. Most people weren't supposed to reach the age of 65 back then, so the Social Security retirement age was set at 65. Boy, things have sure changed.

So, here I am at age 88, like so many others, well beyond retirement age. What do I do? A lot of us have hobbies. I have a brother-in-law that golfs a lot. Sometimes he goes to golf conventions, and sometimes he plays two rounds of golf in one day. He told me if it weren't for golf, he would have nothing to do. I hear this repeated a lot: "If it weren't for golf…" He was a champion salesperson before retirement, and I wonder how he could have used those skills today.

In Florida, many homes are on golf courses, including mine. But I'm not a golfer; I am a woodturner. My great joy is making beautiful gifts out of wood. I like to take a wooden bowl as a hostess gift rather than a bottle of wine. Even though I spend a lot of time turning wood, I still have additional time for my favorite ministry.

At a CBMC function at Glen Eyrie, Colorado, I was introduced to the Pocket Testament League many years ago. What do they do? They share the Gospel of John with folks they meet. I was fascinated by the Pocket Testament League but did nothing about it until about six years ago. When God brought up that old memory, I ordered my first thirty pocket testaments and started sharing them. Their motto is "Read, Carry, Share." Everywhere I go, I look for opportunities to share a pocket testament with those who serve me in the community and others to engage in conversation.

A year ago, my wife Elaine and I went to a furniture store to purchase a chair. I had a pocket testament in my shirt pocket and gave it to the salesperson. It gave me an excellent opportunity to share the gift of salvation with her. She said she was interested in spiritual things and had been looking for a church. Last week we went back to the same store, and we asked for the same clerk. A year later, she still had the pocket testament clipped to her clipboard. Our conversation once again turned to spiritual things. She said she reads the Bible consistently and now is a regular attendee of a Bible-teaching church.

So, whenever I go out, I put at least three testaments in my pocket. We have a large Hispanic population, and I carry one Spanish/English copy. I joke with my wife that when I have given out all three pocket testaments, we can go home!

Bottom Line: I have found a way to live out my faith in my retirement by creatively connecting my daily tasks with intentional conversations. Even a trip to Walmart can be exciting. What are you doing to be intentional with your time each day? Maybe you, too, should check out the Pocket Testament League that I mentioned above at www.PTL.org.

## Chapter 4 Questions

1. Name someone that has mentored you.

2. Is there someone that would consider you a mentor?

3. Ted finds intentionality in his daily routine. He builds time into his errands for engaging people in conversations and giving them a Gospel of John. He uses his age and interests to break down barriers. Are you willing to do that, too?

# 5

## iRetire4Him:
## Mentor in Action

RETIREMENT IS THE BEGINNING of an adventure. When you make mentoring others the mission of your retirement adventure, you will experience excitement and add challenge to your day. If you are one of the many retirees who miss their work's daily challenges, you can find it while mentoring.

Martha and I have been marriage mentors for about twenty years. Mostly our time is invested in couples about two decades younger than us. We have learned many things about mentoring couples. Here are just a few. You can't care about a couple's marriage more than they do. Many younger married couples do not have a successful marriage in their family to look at as an example. The couples we mentor can learn just as much from our wisdom and our mistakes. Impromptu time with a couple is just as valuable as planned out couple mentoring. Mentoring couples has

> *Iron sharpens iron, and one man sharpens another.*
> *—Proverbs 27:17 ESV*

strengthened our marriage, and many of the mentor couples have become lifelong friends. Being a mentor isn't always easy, but it is still rewarding. Maybe you aren't up to mentoring married couples, so here are some practical ideas for putting your faith, abilities, and energy into action in investing in the next generation through mentoring.

## Mentoring Idea Number One: Playing Games, Babysitting, and Changing Lives

Playing board games and card games is a powerful relationship-building tool for family and friends. Some think playing board games and card games is a lost pass time in our internet-based world, but all of our kids and spouses regularly play board games. During the pandemic, board game playing became a favorite pastime while we are stuck at home. What do we gain by playing games with our families and friends? Games help us grow relationships. When playing games, conversations abound, especially competitive banter. Very few even realize that friendships are being forged discussing real issues while the games proceeds.

When playing games with your younger neighbors, kids, and grandkids, offer to supply some home-cooked food as an added attraction. When my kids had friends over, they loved having a real meal around a dinner table. Most of them never experienced that at home. Those kids are now in their 30s, and it's still the same.

We have found that younger adults love to interact with people older than themselves. When Martha and I make ourselves available to the couples we mentor, they gladly take the time to hang out with us. They seek answers to questions and want the wisdom we have to offer. We find the most powerful place to talk in our home continues to be the dinner table where you face each other and engage in conversations. If the couples you invite over have children, invite them too. If the couple you are spending time with desires a little "no kid" time, offer to pay for a babysitter.

Paying for a babysitter is very expensive and often gets in the way of a couple having a date night. Another way Martha and I found to minister to the couples we mentor is to offer to babysit. It's not my favorite thing, but it really makes a difference for the couple and the kids. Most of the couples we mentor don't have healthy relationships with their parents, so their kids don't get much exposure to grandparent-aged people. It is a joy to love on these kids when they are in our home. It is also nice to send them home with Mom and Dad.

> *Live wisely among those who are not believers, and make the most of every opportunity.*
> *—Colossians 4:5 NLT*

Being intentional regularly will result in you gaining influence in their lives. Earn their trust, play games, and eat food. It's a recipe for success. Monopoly anyone? (Star Wars Edition, of course.)

## Mentoring Idea Number Two: House Repairs— Normal to You but Intimidating to Many

Changing light bulbs, changing furnace filters, painting a room, changing the oil, and fixing a leaky faucet are projects that are on honey-do lists everywhere. The list may not intimidate you because regular repairs are part of what you grew up doing. Many people, in the next generations, need to learn how to maintain and repair a home. Sure, they can try to learn on YouTube, but how much better would it be if you volunteered to work alongside them and show them what a joy it is to fix things with their own two hands.

I find that confidence builds when you work shoulder-to-shoulder. Martha and I have helped many couples paint rooms, organize garages, fix electrical, clean cabinets, and so many more things. Most couples we mentor don't have family nearby, so they are grateful for the extra help.

I remember one couple, the Johnsons, in particular. We had been mentoring the Johnsons formally for about six months. The wife, who was homeschooling and raising five kids, was overwhelmed and couldn't seem to get her house in order. The husband was frustrated, but he didn't know how to proceed. We volunteered to come over to their home on a Saturday to work as a family and clean out the place. At the end of the day, with all the kids helping, the house was in order, a dumpster was filled, a load went to the thrift store, and 37 odd socks met their demise. The Johnson kids had a blast, and one of these kids is now married, and we are mentoring him and his wife. Being a mentor is such a blessing to Martha and me. We had so much fun that day.

Many different couples have mentored Martha and me, but two couples in our lives made a huge difference: Martha's sister Diana and her husband John, and my sister Sue and her husband, Jeff. These two brothers-in-law aren't afraid to try to fix anything. With them around, I am not scared to try to fix anything either. That's mentoring.

When I was a kid, my dad taught me how to paint—first a room, then a set of rooms, then we painted the house, then I painted a house with Martha. Every time you learn how to fix something on your own, you build confidence and save money. Mentoring is dripping your life on another, one drop at a time.

When you help someone with a project around the house, it is natural to engage in thoughtful conversations. Your relationship with them grows deeper because you are investing in them. Ask yourself: what skill or knowledge do I have that someone younger would like to learn? Wax a car? Fix an electrical outlet? Clean a house? Helping someone better themselves with an investment of your time makes a lifelong impact.

Your intentionality to help the younger generation will mean the world to them. Do it together and watch

> *Don't be selfish; don't try to impress others. Be humble, thinking of others as better than yourselves.*
> *—Philippians 2:3 NLT*

your impact grow. Whenever you help someone get a project done, celebrate the completed work. If a free meal or dessert is offered, graciously accept it as a gift of thanks. It makes them feel like they paid you back, and you get to test a new recipe.

## Mentoring Idea Number Three: Hanging Out and Taking Day Trips

Spending time with someone is valuable, no matter what you are doing. As your relationship builds with the people you have been mentoring, talk with them about taking a trip. Everyone is busy these days, but everyone also needs a break and adventure too. A trip doesn't have to be overnight. It could be a trip to the local pond for some fishing or a trip to a local market to do some window shopping. A trip takes us away from our daily routine and makes a relaxed conversation possible.

The time you spend as a mentor needs to be relaxed and fun, but it is also a platform for you to engage in conversations that lead to faith and life. This time with them in a casual, fun atmosphere allows you to introduce them to the Author of our faith and the Giver of our life. It takes time to build the trust to have that conversation. Frankly, it takes time to convince those younger than us to hang out with us. That is why ideas one and two are focused on spending time with others. You can get started doing that right away.

Over time, you can build enough trust to spend the day together. Think about all the great little trips you can take on a Saturday morning. Trips to car shows, flea markets, craft fairs, fruit festivals, carnivals, holiday celebrations, boat parades, camper and RV shows, etc. These are great little three or four-hour trips during which you can share some of your life with them, and they can learn about life from you.

The trip doesn't have to end at a tourist destination. It could be a trip to a store where you need some "help" picking something up or dropping something off. It could also be a trip to the mechanic where you need to drop off your car. Think about buying them a coffee on the way as a thank you for helping. Every way you spend time with someone of the next generation, the time is well spent. I have heard couples and young men say it to me. At the end of this book, there is an article about Grant Skeldon. He wrote an entire book about the millennial generation wanting to walk alongside the generations that came before them. You will be blessed when you spend time as a mentor and hanging out with young folks will also help you feel younger.

So, take a trip and drag your mentee along with you. No matter how old you are, there is always someone younger nearby that can use a reliable mentor and friend. You will be able to share knowledge, wisdom, and eventually about your friend Jesus. Ask the Lord to give you creative ideas to engage and build relationships with the next generations.

## Mentoring Idea Number Four: Share Your Successes and Failures in a Crowd

Many of you are designed by God to be small group leaders, younger married class sponsors, marriage mentors, or guest speakers at marriage retreats. You have a lifetime of experience in marriage, budgeting, debt management, learning stewardship, raising children, and family relationships. There is nothing more rewarding than investing your life into a group of people who need to know what you know. When you are willing to hang out with groups of young people, this gives you access to lots of couples at one time. You can let them know you are available and build relationships with them over time.

Our friends, Dick and Karen, are in their 70s. For the last 30 years, they have intentionally hung out with college-aged and young married people. Their favorite hobby is marriage mentoring. They deliberately put themselves in the place of influence on the lives of those who genuinely need them. It's an excellent example for us all to follow. Dick and Karen have proven over and over how significant the need is for mentors. Will you consider responding to that need as well? I guarantee there is a need for you in a group somewhere near you. It could be at church or a local community center. Sometimes you just have to ask, "Does someone around here need a mentor or mentor couple?" Being a mentor will change your life and the life of your mentee. Titus 2:1 says, "As for you, Titus, promote the kind of living that reflects wholesome teaching" (NLT).

## Ted Hains Shares a Story: Trains, Pains, and Tools – Back at it Again

I had just spent 41 years in photography, and it was time to retire. I sold my portrait studio in 1998.

I had been dabbling in garden railroads (G-scale trains about the size of a bread box). I built my backyard railroad intending to be the best in the Garden Railroad Club. I used thyme dispersed throughout my village to look like little trees, and I had a giant lake with bridges running across it. I had a section that looked like a farming community, representing my grandfather Hahn's farm. My setup also had a small town with a grocery store, representing my grandmother Hains's store. My garden railroad was complete, and I could finally host the Garden Railroad Club open house at my home.

I played with my train until it was a magnificent structure, including train cars and an engine from the Rock Island Railroad. I felt that I had the most fantastic backyard railroad in the Minneapolis-Saint Paul region.

But soon after I completed it, arthritis in my knees made it difficult for me to kneel and repair a track or put a train back on the track.

One day Elaine, my wife, pointed out to me that I had gotten very dull. She said I needed some "outside" stimulation. I had always worked with people, and I enjoy being with them, but I had isolated myself with this passion for building my railroad.

The answer was to get a job. I had always enjoyed working with wood, so I applied to the Rockler Woodworking store in Burnsville, Minnesota. I got an $8.50 an hour sales job with a 20% discount on tools. A wonderful deal! On payday, I usually went home with a new tool. I had a blast. People would come in with problems, and I would help them solve them. Usually, they needed a tool they did not have to solve their problem. To be successful in their project, I would sell them a new tool. This job felt like a win-win for me. I worked in an environment with tools, something I enjoyed, and they even paid me to do it. I helped people with problems, and my boss was happy because I was selling his tools. Occasionally, I was able to share about Jesus too.

Bottom Line: Pleasure only satisfies so long. I was made to work. I found satisfying work, and it has created a lifelong passion for woodworking. Retirement was just a pivoting point in my life, heading me in a different direction. I wasn't washed up, I was just finishing one phase of life and moving on to another. What about you? Have you matched your talents with your time to gain fulfillment in retirement?

# Chapter 5 Questions

1. Which mentoring idea are you willing to tackle first?

2. Teaching cooking, cleaning, and house maintenance are just a few. What every day skill can you use to open the doors for a next-generation relationship?

3. Ted developed a hobby with his backyard garden model railroad. When he first retired, he thought that investing time in perfecting his display would bring him fulfillment. He was wrong. What hobby have you expected to satisfy you? Is it working?

4. Ted went back to work with a whole new perspective in retirement. Have you considered going back to work? Why or why not?

# 6

## iRetire4Him: Working

MANY RETIREES WORK DURING their retirement years. Some work for money out of necessity and some out of desire. Some work as a regular volunteer. Work brings pleasure, so it is no wonder many retirees re-enter the workforce. Going back to work is an opportunity to provide a fresh perspective. You may no longer desire to work in the career you were in for decades, but you still might have the desire to work. You have skills and experiences from which others can benefit. Any way you look at it, going back to work provides you a fresh opportunity to live out the iRetire4Him lifestyle.

Ask yourself a few questions.

- How can you work with intentionality in your new position (for pay or volunteer)?

- How will this experience be different than the years you spent working hard for a paycheck?

- What difference do you want to make to those you work alongside?

For those of you ready to earn a paycheck, take this opportunity to research culture before committing to an organization. The company culture must appreciate what a mature worker can bring to the team. To experience the most impact from your intentional desire to be employed, work in an environment that will treat you well and appreciate your fit within the organization. Don't rush into this. Many companies and organizations would love to have you on their team.

If you are looking to volunteer, take time to research the organization's mission and culture before committing your time. Nonprofits are often underfunded and overwhelmed and would love to have a volunteer with skills like yours. Don't just look to Christian organizations but look at all organizations making a difference in the community. Find one that focuses on a community problem you feel drawn to solve. If you volunteer for a secular nonprofit, you get to be a light for Christ in that organization. That's huge.

*You can be a vital part of the organization.*

Whether you earn a paycheck or become a steady volunteer, you can be a vital part of the organization. Your work will keep your mind sharp, use your skills, and allow you to invest in the next generation. Assessing the work environment is critical for a working retiree. Finding a culture that will embrace you and allow a rich and encouraging experience is vital to your success.

Now that you've chosen to work at a specific organization, let's develop a lifestyle of intentionality at work, whether you go to work every day, every other day, or just once a week. How do you bring your faith and put it into action as you learn to iRetire4Him in a new work-place? It is time to put Chapter 3 into action.

*Step 1:* Get to know the people you work alongside. Learn their names. You can use a notebook to track what you learn—note details about their family, hobbies, and how they spend their time after work. Engage them in conversation to build trust. It will take time to build trust, and some will be skeptical. They may not be accustomed to having relationships with older generations. Love them and get to know them.

*Step 2:* Look for ways to serve those around you in a way that your job description doesn't require you to serve. If you're volunteering, that may be easier than if you're getting paid to accomplish a specific job. Look for additional ways to help the people around you. Listen to them and learn where they are struggling. Pay attention to what they don't understand within their jobs. By being a good listener, you can find a way to serve them in a significant and meaningful way.

*Step 3:* Spend time together outside of the work environment, away from the pressures of work. This step requires a little more boldness on your part. Keep in mind that it's going to take some time to get to this step. Getting together with our work friends outside of our workplace can take the friendship to a whole new level. It takes time to develop their trust. Try inviting co-workers for a cup of coffee after work or eat lunch with them at work. Over time, you can generate enough trust to ask them to your home for a meal.

It's essential to use discretion when inviting others into your home. Prayer is a powerful tool for discernment. If you live alone or are single, try meeting at a local diner for coffee or a meal. Offering to treat is a sure way to get a meal with your workmates. You have years of wisdom under your belt; it's time to share that wisdom. The whole idea is to get some time with people outside of the work environment to develop your relationship's depth. That depth gives you a chance to share the hope that you have in Jesus.

*Step 4:* Pray with others. Prayer is powerful. God is at work in our work, so involve Him in the conversation. Asking a co-worker how they are doing is a critical element in developing a relationship with them. The key is to listen to their answer. When we take the time to ask the question, "How are you doing?" we need to stop and wait for the reply. Let them give you a real answer. If they happen to share about adversity in their lives, it's a great time to ask the next question: "Can I pray for you about that right now?" I can't point to a time in the last 15 years that anybody has ever said, "No." If they share a struggle, they are often looking for a solution, and prayer may bring the answer they need. Pray a short and simple prayer and ask for Jesus to give them an answer to their prayers. Don't be afraid, and don't be ashamed. Praying with a co-worker is a powerful tool of God in the workplace.

*Step 5:* Do your work with excellence. The tasks you commit to accomplishing as an employee or a volunteer should be excellent. Only agree to do things that you know you can do well. As we age, we may have additional limitations, especially physically. Be realistic with what you agree to do. Our excellence displays our connection to our Heavenly Father, and it is a blessing to our co-workers and employers. If you need help, don't be afraid or ashamed to ask. Be open to training and seek advice from those around you. It endears people to you when you show that you need them as much as they need you. Be diligent in making sure your work is excellent and would make anyone proud, especially your Heavenly Father.

These five steps will help you live with intentionality in the work or volunteer place of your retirement years. If you're going to be at work, you might as well look at it as a mission field filled with ministry opportunities. All five steps above will enable you to use that mission field for God's glory and open conversations about Jesus. You can accomplish the Great Commission while you are completing work and making some extra cash. It's the best of both worlds. Have fun and realize that the people around you desperately need to meet Jesus, and you may be their only chance of making that happen.

## Ted Hains Shares a Story: On Vacation and Mentoring a Neighbor

After I sold my photography studio in 1998, we lived in Savage, Minnesota, in a beautiful one-story home. It was getting to be too much to care for the large garden and my garden railroad.

Elaine and I were looking at our next phase of life. We were about to put the deposit on a lovely senior living high rise when I concluded living there would be stifling. The following day, I said to Elaine, "I have always wanted to live on a lake. I am 72, and if we're ever going to do it, that time is now."

For several years, we had driven about four hours north of Minneapolis to Anglers Beach on Cass Lake in the center of the Ojibway National Forest. The summer of 2006 was the last time Anglers Beach would be open. The only cabin available was an old trailer in very poor shape. Our daughter, Diana, told us about a nearby resort being developed for individual ownership of lots and cabins. She thought we might want to live there since it was near-by. We checked it out, and we loved it. The resort was right on the lake, and we put our money down. We ordered a factory-built cabin that was about 1,200 square feet and decided that it would be the perfect place to spend our summers.

The cabin next door was being built at the same time by a Minneapolis foot surgeon named Jim, his wife, and their four teenagers. Their side door and our front door were only 20 feet apart. Consequently, we saw them a lot when they were there on weekends.

Jim and I had many conversations as we went in and out of our respective cabins. I soon found out that Jim was a devout Roman Catholic and his brother-in-law was a priest. We often talked about spiritual things, and Jim would ask me questions about the Bible and woodwork-ing, as I had a nice shop in my garage. I had built a natural edge table and sofa table. Jim asked if I could help him build a sofa table for his cabin. I jumped at the chance. We found the appropriate timber with a natural edge. I helped him by guiding him with what he needed to do next. During that time, we talked about Jesus a lot. We could only work on this project a little bit each weekend when he came up, so we had to strategize our time.

One of those weekends, Jim called me on his way home from the cabin. He said, "I have kind of a strange request to make of you. Would you consider being my spiritual mentor?" I didn't have to think about that at all. I responded, "Of course, I would be honored." We decided to do some Bible studies. We started with the book of John in the New Testament. It is an ideal place to start for any-one on a fresh spiritual journey. Jim had not read the Bible much, so I asked him if he would like one like mine, a New Living Translation version. He said yes, and I got him one as a gift. We went through many books together as he had many questions. If I didn't know the answer, I had several good commentaries for reference. Jim told me once he would never become anything but a Catholic, and he loved the sacraments. I said, "Is Jesus your Lord and Savior?" Jim answered, "Yes." "Cool," I said. Jim became my best friend. Jim shares his love for Jesus with other doctors in their practices.

Because I spend my winters in Florida, it is challeng-ing to do Bible studies together, but we do so by phone on occasion. I wanted to write this article about Jim and our relationship. I didn't want to do it without asking him first, so last night, I called him and told him that we were starting this new thing called iRetire4Him and how people in retirement years should actively share Christ.

Jim listened, and I could hear a choke in his voice as he said, "This is amazing! Just Friday, I was sitting in my chair and didn't have much to do, so I drove in my car, not knowing where I was going but found myself circling my church. It was then that I realized *I could do something for the church.*" Jim had done landscaping while in school, and he still had some pretty good equipment. He said, "I could clean up the shrubs, trim the trees, mow the lawn, and shovel the snow." Wow, I thought, that would get him talking to other people and sharing Christ.

We have now been at our cabin for 15 years, and Elaine and I are often called upon for prayer before our association has any function that serves food. They have recognized God is at the center of our lives. Elaine's been quilting all this time and shares her gifts and Jesus with the ladies in our neighborhood. Many of these ladies are Christ-followers, enjoy quilting, and share by praying for each other. Last summer, Elaine said to me, "I love this place." We have learned that our "lifestyle" of loving people helps them to see Christ in us and to want the same thing in their own lives.

Bottom Line: I saw a need in a friend for a deeper spiritual walk. Jim saw in me something he wanted to have. I invested in him, and then Jim went on to invest in his doctor friends and now his local church. I learned that loving my neighbors is one of the most powerful things I can do. It's easy too. How about you? Do you know your neighbors all around you? Do they know you? Retirement is the best time to invest in those relationships. What can you do today to minister to a neighbor? It doesn't have to start with preaching a sermon. Just start with a smile and a friendly conversation. See where it leads from there.

## Chapter 6 Questions

1. Do you miss working? How will you choose to re-engage the job culture with the iRetire4Him lifestyle?

2. List some local non-profit organizations that you love and are willing to serve as a volunteer?

3. Ted developed a relationship with a neighbor up at his lake cabin. This relationship led his friend to a deeper relationship with Christ. What can you do to start intentional conversations with your neighbors?

# 7

## iRetire4Him: Costs

*Don't copy the behavior and customs of this world,
but let God transform you into a new person by
changing the way you think.*

—Rom. 12:2 NLT

THINGS OF VALUE HAVE a cost. Moving near our kids and away from longtime friends has a cost. Suppose you decide to leave your small group to be in a church with your kids and grandkids. This decision has a cost too. Each of these costs has a benefit, but it also involves sacrifice. When we give up something for Jesus, the cost of following Him has long term benefits.

> *Things of value have a cost.*

My time following Jesus revealed seven costs that all of us must face if we are going to iRetire4Him. You may experience different costs in committing your retirement to the Lord. I know there will be costs, but every cost you face will be worth it.

Scripture sets the stage to learn about worthy costs. In Romans 12:2 above, Paul says you need to let God transform you into a new person, by changing the way you think. As we read, pray, grow, and learn, it's essential to allow God to be the transformer. He will help us to think like Him and not like the world. In Matthew 5–7, Jesus laid out the costs of following Him in our retirement when He preached the Sermon on the Mount. Take a few minutes right now to grab your Bible and read those chapters before you go any further here. Note the costs and the benefits that Jesus mentions.

## Cost #1: Give Up Wrong Thoughts

Sinful thoughts run freely in our minds and afflict many of us. Jesus addressed this issue head-on in Matthew 23:27 when he called out the Pharisees and labeled them whitewashed tombs. They looked good on the outside, but they were dead inside. Our sinful thoughts can leave us dead inside too. The good news is that Jesus is there to help us with these thoughts through the Holy Spirit. As you learn to follow Jesus in a way that influences those you hang out with in retirement, it's no longer an option to look good outside but be a mess inside.

> But I warn you—unless your righteousness is better than the righteousness of the teachers of religious law and the Pharisees, you will never enter the Kingdom of Heaven! (Matt. 5:20 NLT)

Our wrong thoughts cause us to drift away from where God wants us to be. Giving up wrong thoughts may seem simple, but it can be the most difficult to do. My wrong thoughts are often judgmental. I pray about it, and

I think I am doing better until I get behind the wheel of a car, and the judging comes out again.

Just the other day, I was on the main road here in Ft. Myers, Florida, and a driver in front of me made a left turn from the right-hand turn lane. I find myself talking to these people out loud in my car. I criticize their driving and call them names. It's possible they were lost and realized it at the last minute, but a safe U-turn would have been a better option. Talking about others behind my car's wheel is just one way I find myself having negative thoughts. I also speak to the newscasters on TV. They churn up all kinds of viciousness inside of me. That's my story, what is yours? Where do you find yourself being critical and having ugly thoughts about people?

When I judge people, I often miss who the real person is on the inside. Once we get to know an individual, as an image-bearer of God, we see His amazing hand in their lives. Getting to know people may not be possible when you drive down the road, but it is possible with those in your neighborhood, church, or community center.

Judging others may not be your thought-based struggle, but whatever your mind battle is, God wants to bring you internal healing. A clean mind is a place God can use more effectively in your retirement mission field. iRetire4Him is a lifestyle and a statement of faith and giving up wrong thoughts is one way to put that faith into action.

Re-read Romans 12:2 and see the miracle God provides for our minds.

> Don't copy the behavior and customs of this world, but let God transform you into a new person by *changing the way you think*. Then you

will learn to know God's will for you, which is good and pleasing and perfect. (NLT, emphasis added)

Our thinking can change, and this verse tells us that God can do that. We can hear the very voice of God. Let go of the old way of thinking and watch your faith grow.

## Cost #2: Give Up a Double Life

As Christ-followers, consistency in our behavior should be a hallmark of our lives. We should be the same person wherever we go, honoring Jesus all the time. I used to live one way on Sunday and Wednesday night and another way for the rest of the week.

As a young manager, one of my direct reports was a single mom, who often had kid distractions at work. She was a believer and knew I was too, but there was conflict. She said I was condescending and arrogant, and unfortunately, I was. One day her car broke down, and I used my expertise to get her a great deal on another vehicle. After helping her, she remarked, "Jim, why are you being so nice to me?" She was referring to my double life. At work, I was a jerk. Outside of work, I let my faith loose and served others. I have never been the same since she spoke those words into my life. I have tried to find her recently to ask forgiveness for the pain I caused her but haven't been successful yet.

Are you struggling with living a double life? Some of the most valuable human qualities include authenticity, transparency, and vulnerability. Jesus consistently demonstrated these qualities, and we can too. When we have a conflict with our neighbors that goes unresolved, and then we go to church on Sunday, our neighbors notice. Pre-believers have a way of expecting us "church-going religious folks" always to do the right thing. Our behavior gets seen. If it doesn't match up, it causes some people to discount the power of Jesus. Does your behavior in your everyday life match up with your behavior on Sunday? Pre-believers can tell a phony from a mile away, and living a double life is fake.

Authentic living allows others to see the work God is doing in our lives. Pre-believers will notice when you love your neighbor and reconcile with them. When they see you living differently from the world, they will want to know why. Then you get to tell them about how Jesus saved you and is working on you day by day. When we put aside our pride and openly show our struggles, we attract broken people. The Apostle Paul did this well, and he wrote about it in many of his books in the New Testament. He talked a ton about it in Romans Chapter 7.

Here is Jesus's perspective:

> You are the light of the world—like a city on a hilltop that cannot be hidden. No one lights a lamp and then puts it under a basket. Instead, a lamp is placed on a stand, where it gives light to everyone in the house. In the same way, let your good deeds shine out for all to see, so that everyone will praise your heavenly Father.
> (Matt. 5:14–16 NLT)

# Cost #3: Give Up Unforgiveness

Unforgiveness defined the first 40 years of my life as I struggled with bitterness and anger. It is often said and attributed to many different people that bitterness is like a poison pill we take, hoping our enemy will die. I took that pill for years. Bitterness is perhaps the most self-destructive human emotion. It can impact your health and keep others from wanting to be around you. The root is often unforgiveness, and unforgiveness had ruled my life.

Forgiveness is something most Christ-followers take for granted. We love the fact that we are all forgiven by Jesus. But when someone sins against us, we don't want to extend the same grace, even if they are family, friends, or neighbors.

Read what Jesus says about it:

> But I say, love your enemies! Pray for those who persecute you! In that way, you will be acting as true children of your Father in heaven. For he gives his sunlight to both the evil and the good, and he sends rain on the just and the unjust alike. If you love only those who love you, what reward is there for that? Even corrupt tax collectors do that much. If you are kind only to your friends, how are you different from anyone else? Even pagans do that. But you are to be perfect, even as your Father in heaven is perfect. (Matt. 5:44–48 NLT)

> If you forgive those who sin against you, your
> heavenly Father will forgive you. But if you re-
> fuse to forgive others, your Father will not for-
> give your sins. (Matt. 6:14–15 NLT)

Why is giving up unforgiveness a cost related to living out the iRetire4Him lifestyle? Forgiveness is the hallmark of Jesus's rescue plan for humanity. When we demonstrate forgiveness to those who have hurt us, we show in a small way what God is offering every human on the planet.

Think of the impact on those we live alongside in our retirement when we demonstrate forgiveness. Many of us know what it is like to work in a place governed by grudges and unforgiveness. We call that a toxic work environment. What is it like to live in a neighborhood where grudges and unforgiveness abound? We call that neighborhood blight. When we forgive those who hurt us and ask forgiveness of those we hurt, we replace toxicity with love. When we learn to demonstrate this in our neighborhoods, churches, and community centers, it gets noticed.

Martha was the president of our homeowner's association for ten years. As the president, she worked hard to eliminate annoying rules and work through issues that brought conflict. As a couple, we worked hard to build friendships and share unconditional love with our neighbors by serving each of them uniquely. There were only 30 units in the neighborhood, so we knew everyone. But there were many times someone in the community was mean to Martha. When this happened, I got angry. One time, I communicated my anger to this person and acted like a three-year-old. I disagreed with this man's behavior, but mine was worse because I knew better. I had to apologize and ask forgiveness for the things I said. Showing outward love for someone who was openly a local Scrooge was hard, but it was necessary. Jesus taught us to love our enemies and pray for those who persecute you. I had to learn that the hard way because people in the neighborhood knew I was a believer. I performed marriages and funerals for my neighbors. They expected to see Jesus in me, and they were watching.

Jesus came to set us all free from the bondage of sin. He wants us to let go of the bitterness and hurt so we can be set free and lead others to freedom. When we do, it attracts others to Jesus. Everyone around us wants to be free from bitterness and pain; your life will show them how to be free when you model forgiveness.

Forgiveness isn't easy, but it can be simple. If we believe and act on Jesus's words from Matthew 5 and 6, it will change the way we think. He was serious about forgiveness, and now it's our turn.

## Cost #4: Give Up Damaged Relationships

My past is peppered with damaged relationships. For years, I counted on future opportunities to make new friends instead of dealing with the pain of resolving conflict. I moved on from broken relationships, pretending it didn't bother me, but they were hindering the growth of my faith and my reputation as a follower of Jesus.

The world is small, and I often encounter people from my past. I realized it was time to walk the path of reconciliation, deal with the hurt, and repair relationships.

I prayed and asked God to reveal the relationship carnage of my past; the list was long. I reached out to people and asked for forgiveness. Some responded positively, some reacted negatively, and some didn't respond. In 2005, I destroyed a 20-year-old relationship. My friend had hurt me, and instead of talking it through, I stormed out and launched a verbal torpedo. Later, the Lord reminded me of all the great things this one friend had brought into my life. I was humbled and tried to call him, but his phone number changed. I sent a letter asking forgiveness and thanked him for all the great ways God had used him in my life. I never heard back, but I know that I said what needed to be said. My actions caused hurt. I could have set an example back in 2005 by seeking to have an adult conversation, but instead, I destroyed a relationship.

Pre-believers are watching Christ-followers and our relationships. If our relationships look broken and dysfunctional, just like the worlds, what hope do we offer them? Jesus came to heal broken relationships, especially the one with our Heavenly Father. As you live out your faith in your retirement, consider reconciling with those with whom you have damaged relationships. Seek to repair old relationships, which may involve reconciling with family, kids, grandkids, former co-workers, neighbors, people from church, and anyone else you've hurt.

Jesus expects peaceful resolution and reconciliation in the relationships of his followers. When we demonstrate reconciliation in our own lives, people will begin to experience Jesus through you. When you ask forgiveness of all the people you have hurt in the past, you will experience unprecedented freedom. Jesus talked about repairing relationships in Matthew 5.

> So if you are presenting a sacrifice at the altar in the Temple and you suddenly remember that someone has something against you, leave your sacrifice there at the altar. Go and be reconciled to that person. Then come and offer your sacrifice to God. (Matt. 5:23–24 NLT)

Ask God to reveal damaged relationships from your past. Someone probably came to mind as soon as you read this sentence. Typically, these are the people you argue with in your head. When God reveals a damaged relationship, quickly try to bring forgiveness into the relationship. You will find healing for yourself and others when repairing damaged relationships.

## Cost #5: Give Up Hoarding Wealth

A hoarder is someone who keeps it all for himself. It's a worldly trait, not a biblical one. As followers of Jesus, we are to live generously as Jesus did. He demonstrated the ultimate generosity when He gave up His life for you and me. Hoarding keeps us from experiencing the joy of generosity, and it puts a roadblock in your testimony in retirement.

After Martha and I had been married for almost 13 years, we took a class on the biblical principles of money and possessions from Crown Financial Ministry. The course taught us, "You have been blessed 'financially,' not to increase your status of living but to increase your status of giving." This statement is not bashing people who have nice stuff. It is a statement of caution to Christ-followers to keep money from becoming their master.

Martha and I had to learn to live with an open hand. In our car business, we made it a practice to be generous with our repairs and maintenance. We found freedom in giving extra, even when it went unnoticed. When a customer asked why we went above and beyond, it allowed us to share our values.

You may be asking yourself, what does this have to do with iRetire4Him. Jesus modeled generosity. A life of generosity will enable you to experience independence from your possessions. Jesus came to set us free. Free from sin and free from allowing possessions to own us. Generosity is a way to be truly free.

Generosity looks different for each person. For some, it may mean sharing your money or possessions. For others, it may mean sharing your time and expertise. Each one of us has wealth hidden inside of us, just bursting to get out. The Holy Spirit of God lives in you as a Christ-follower, and He will equip you to be generous. You only have to be willing. Generosity attracts people to Jesus.

Jesus said it best in Matthew 6.

> Don't store up treasures here on earth, where moths eat them and rust destroys them, and where thieves break in and steal. Store your treasures in heaven, where moths and rust cannot destroy, and thieves do not break in and steal. Wherever your treasure is, there the desires of your heart will also be... No one can serve two masters. For you will hate one and

love the other; you will be devoted to one and despise the other. You cannot serve God and be enslaved to money. (Matt. 6:19–21, 24 NLT)

## Cost #6: Give Up Worry

At 19 years old, I memorized the following passage from Matthew 6. Little did I know how much that would help me later in life.

> Therefore I tell you, do not worry about your life, what you will eat or drink; or about your body, what you will wear. Is not life more than food, and the body more than clothes? Look at the birds of the air; they do not sow or reap or store away in barns, and yet your heavenly Father feeds them. Are you not much more valuable than they? Can any one of you by worrying add a single hour to your life?
>
> And why do you worry about clothes? See how the flowers of the field grow. They do not labor or spin. Yet I tell you that not even Solomon in all his splendor was dressed like one of these. If that is how God clothes the grass of the field, which is here today and tomorrow is thrown into the fire, will he not much more clothe you—you of little faith? So do not worry, saying, "What shall we eat?" or "What shall we drink?" or "What shall we wear?" For the pagans run after all these things, and your heavenly Father knows that you need them. But seek first his kingdom and his righteousness,

and all these things will be given to you as
well. Therefore do not worry about tomorrow,
for tomorrow will worry about itself. Each day
has enough trouble of its own. (Matt 6:25–34
NIV)

Martha and I have lived in Florida for almost twenty
years. It is one of the retirement meccas of our great country. Nearly all of our neighbors are retired. We hear worry
from them all the time: worry about their money lasting to
their final days, worry about their kids and grandkids,
worry about politics, worry about association dues, worry
about their church, and worry about their health. It's a
whole lot of worry. Does worry dominate your conversations too? Worry should not define us. We should defy
worry.

Our lives as Christ-followers are supposed to be defined by a new way of living and thinking. Worry is the
old way, not the new way. Jesus said He would take care
of us, and He will. The Bible is full of stories of provision,
and He is still providing today. About three years ago,
Martha and I desperately needed a newer vehicle for travel. Our neighbors all knew our van was aging with over
250,000 miles on it. They also knew we couldn't afford to
buy a new car. When we drove home a ten-year-newer
van into our neighborhood, everyone wanted to know the
story. They all found out about God's amazing provision
through a bunch of donors. They saw God's hand at work.
Worry was replaced by trust. Trust in the one who created
it all and said He would provide everything we need. Do
you have a miraculous story of provision to tell?

When we find ourselves worrying, it sends the wrong message to those around us. When we worry, we communicate to others that we doubt the power of God. When we demonstrate our trust in the Almighty God of the universe, it encourages others. We give others a glimpse of His eternal love and provision by not worrying but wearing our belief in God for all to see.

We can deny God's power and allow anxiety to rule our lives or trust Him and live in peace. Demonstrating this trust in our lives, especially in our retirement years, attracts people to Jesus.

## Cost #7: Give Up Hurry

Be diligent and productive, but never be in a hurry—don't miss those people the Lord puts in front of you. See the opportunities to serve while walking, shopping, building community, and having lunch with friends or neighbors. People in pain are everywhere, and we can be there for them. Learning not to be in a hurry all the time has been a hard lesson for me. I am always busy and often in a hurry. I have learned that the incidents where people cause me to be late are often the people who most need me now when I am in a hurry.

A few winters ago, Martha and I were out on a date. It was late, and we were in a hurry to get home. On our way home, I noticed something weird on the sidewalk in front of our local citrus grove. I disregarded it and drove on. About a mile later, I said to Martha, "We need to turn around. I think I saw someone on the ground back there." We turned around, parked the car, and walked up the sidewalk to see what was happening. As we approached the scene, we discovered a woman had fallen from her bicycle and was bruised and hurting. She had wrecked her bike and was in no shape to ride home. We put the woman and her bike in our van and took her to her home. We talked with her for a long time. She was hurting and was living in an unpleasant place. She had many addiction issues and uncovered a life damaged in a home where her father never showed her love. We stayed in touch with her for years but eventually lost touch. We got home really late that night but learned never to be in a hurry because someone might need us.

Jesus was always busy but never in a hurry. People were his business. As you learn to live out iRetire4Him as a statement of faith and lifestyle, people are becoming your business, too. You will have opportunities to be like Jesus to people in your retirement if you are available for them. You run into people in your neighborhood, the grocery store, and the parking lot of your church. Do you see them, or are you in too much of a hurry?

Jesus's brother James wrote:

> What good is it, dear brothers and sisters, if you say you have faith but don't show it by your actions? Can that kind of faith save anyone? Suppose you see a brother or sister who has no food or clothing, and you say, "Goodbye and have a good day; stay warm and eat well"—but then you don't give that person any food or clothing. What good does that do? So you see, faith by itself isn't enough. Unless it produces good deeds, it is dead and useless. (Jas. 2:14–17 NLT)

Is your hurried life keeping you from touching the lives of someone who needs to meet Jesus? Take a deep breath and notice the people you connect with all day long. Take time to know them and see what God does next.

There are costs to following Jesus and learning to live out the iRetire4Him lifestyle. Every one of these costs sets us free. We can be free from the bondage of this world and open to do the will of our Heavenly Father. You may have been a Christ-follower for a long time, but you are still learning to follow Jesus. We all are. When we accept the costs of retiring for Him, our lives will be an attraction to pre-believers in our lives, and our relationship with our Heavenly Father will strengthen. The benefit is priceless.

## Ted Hains Shares a Story: The Power of the Pocket Testament

I've been giving out pocket testaments for the past six or seven years, and fewer than ten have ever refused it. As I am headed out for the day, I usually put three or four in my pocket. I pray for the people that are to receive them. It is easier to engage people in conversation than one would think, like talking to people about their children as I am in the checkout line. While talking to them, I usually say, "Here, I'd like you to have this. It's the Gospel of John. Yes, the same John you have in your Bible. I want to share this with you because it has the birth, life, death, and resurrection of Jesus Christ in it." They usually respond with, "Ok, thanks, sir. I'll read it."

One day I stopped at a Wendy's while traveling and gave a pocket testament to the server sitting outside on a curb smoking. I went over to her and said, "I'd like you to have this. It's the Gospel of John." She removed her cigarette to accept the gift. She opened the booklet and began to read as I turned to go my way. I cherish that sight in my memories.

Walmart is one of my favorite places to go. It's easy to engage other shoppers just by asking where the mayonnaise is or the other things guys would typically not be looking for, like baking stuff. Older women are so eager to help! I thank them for their help and say, "I'd like you to have this. It's the Gospel of John." I never hide the fact that it is God's word I'm sharing with them.

Elaine recently asked me to take a fabric package to the postal store to send to one of her friends. I am always looking for the most economical way to get the job done. I was trying to get this fabric into the lowest price USPS box but to no avail. The clerk was watching me and said, "Let me get Josie from the backroom. She is good at this." From the backroom came Josie. With very little trouble, Josie had it in the box in no time! I was impressed. I noticed that she might be Spanish-speaking by her accent, so I said to her, "I'd like to give you this Gospel of John in Spanish and English." Upon receiving it, she nearly jumped over the counter to hug me. I thought, "Wow, how beautiful was her response? I love her enthusiasm."

Another time I was in Walmart standing by the gun case looking at ammunition. I noticed a gentleman with the marine emblem on his cap and a fireman's cross around his neck. I was wearing a hat that had the winged Air Corps emblem on it. I asked him where he had been; he said, "Nam." It seems only a service member can ask other service members about these things. I asked him about his fireman's cross, and he said he had been a volunteer fireman. I handed him a pocket testament and said, "I'd like you to have this. It's God's word." A tear ran down his cheek. He accepted it gladly. I touched his shoulder, and for a long time, two true brothers in Christ from different wars understood.

The Pocket Testament League is my main "go-to" source for starting conversations with people about Jesus. I have been a representative for them for about six years. I like the way individuals receive the pocket testament face-to-face. It's a one-on-one ministry through which you can look the recipient right in the eyes and tell them Jesus loves them.

You, too, can have the joy of sharing Jesus Christ through the Pocket Testament League. Just go to www.PTL.org.

Bottom Line: Retirement has had many surprises for me, and the best surprise is my mission field at Walmart. I love engaging others with God's word, and I love making people smile and cry. Retirement has been energizing and purposeful for me. I live each day with intentionality. What about you? Are you living with purpose in your retirement years?

## Chapter 7 Questions

1. Which cost listed in this chapter was a new idea for you? What are you going to do about it?

2. What cost will be the hardest for you to give up, to live an iRetire4Him lifestyle?

3. Ted regularly finds people ready and willing to accept a part of the Bible as a gift. Which neighbor might be hungry for the truth? Order some pocket testaments today at www. PTL.org and start sharing.

# 8

## iRetire4Him: Lies

IN PURSUING A NEWNESS of life in our retirement, sometimes lies get in our way. The enemy of our soul uses lies to keep us quiet and ineffective in living out our faith and accomplishing the mission given to us by Jesus. For me (Jim), these lies shaped the better part of 40 years of my life. I suspect some of these lies may have shaped your life too.

### Lie #1: My faith impacts only parts of my life.

In my early 20s, two of my mentors spoke this lie into my life. "Work is work, and church is church. They have nothing to do with each other." My mentors didn't mean to teach me this lie. It was modeled to them, and they modeled it to me. That's how the enemy works. He is a deceiver. Work and church, or work and Jesus, have everything to do with each other. But we are talking about our retirement years now. If we turned off Jesus while at work, what other parts of our lives are we tempted to remove from His influence. Does your faith impact the way you play golf, balance your checkbook, play cards with neighbors, or drive your car?

I grew up playing competitive games with my dad: basketball, pool, ping-pong, golf, racquetball, and softball. When I started to get good enough to beat my dad at the game, we stopped playing. My dad is almost eighty-eight now, and we still play pool because he can win most of the time. When my dad developed a cataract in his left eye, he had a blind spot, which I realized while we were playing ping-pong. If I served to the left corner of the table, Dad could never return it. I started beating him wildly, time after time. It felt good to beat him at something, but at what cost? I was taking advantage of him, so I could brag that I won. My faith impacts all of me, even my ping-pong game. When I take advantage of someone to win, what does that say to others around me? I changed my serve and decided to win games volleying with Dad, not taking advantage of him with my serve. It was fair and more fun.

Lie #1 assumes that our faith keeps us from winning and succeeding. The lie asserts that if we live out our faith in Jesus, we will accomplish less because living a life of no compromise would mean settling for less. If you have lived believing this lie, it likely impacted the way you treated people. Don't get caught up in regret. Ask the Lord forgiveness for operating under this lie, and additionally, ask forgiveness from those you took advantage of or mistreated. You can't go back and relive those years with this new knowledge, but you can go forward in retirement with this new understanding and allow it to impact everything you do from now on.

Are you tempted to disconnect your faith in your TV watching, book reading, game playing, neighborhood parties, or homeowner association meetings? All of these activities connect to Jesus as Lord of your life. When we let God shape us, we become more attractive to others to learn about Jesus.

*The truth*: When we follow Jesus, everything connects to our faith.

## Lie #2: Keep your faith at home because of the separation of church and state.

In 1802, Thomas Jefferson wrote a letter to the Danbury Baptist Association about a wall of separation between the church and the state. The intent was to protect the church from the state, not protect the state from the church. You see, Thomas Jefferson understood the government is a threat to the church, and protections need to be in place. However, this protection is misapplied in today's anti-Jesus world. The lies read: "Leave your religion at home. It has no place anywhere outside your home or church building. It does not belong in the government!" Our Founding Fathers formed this country on biblical principles to allow the free expression of religious faith as a core principle for our country. They knew that Jesus and the Bible gave life to all activities of a nation, and our nation without Jesus and the truths of the Bible would be a nation bereft of morality. You have the right to live out your faith everywhere you go. There is no place that you can't take your faith. The United States, without the Church (Jesus), is a mess.

Now that you are retired or contemplating retirement, you may be thinking of how you can use your years of wisdom most effectively. You can run for political office, be on a board of directors or serve in an association. All of these are great places for your faith in Jesus to impact your work.

I have served on many secular boards as a volunteer. I realized that my faith, coupled with my integrity, increased my position of influence. I saw my faith used many times to encourage other believers in the room. My faith opened up doors to pray over meals or pray for a sick member. My volunteer life created more opportunities for me to be Jesus to the pre-believer.

As a representative of Jesus in this world, I know that Jesus provides the only answers to the problems we face. He is the master architect and master healer, too. The people around you need to know this as well. Learn to let your faith flow through you to positively impact others, no matter where you spend your day.

*The truth*: Your faith belongs with you everywhere you go.

## Lie #3: You are a second-tier citizen in the Kingdom of God if you aren't a pastor or missionary.

This lie might sound like this: "If you truly want to make an impact in the Kingdom, then you need to be a pastor or a missionary." Until I was 40, I believed this lie. I felt called to the ministry, so I thought I had to quit my job, go to seminary, and serve in a church somewhere. I believed the lie. I have heard from thousands who also believed the same lie. Did this lie trip you up too?

Lie #3 implies that some positions and responsibilities are more important than others in the Kingdom of God;

that some spiritual gifts are of more importance than other gifts. The truth is, the Kingdom of God has no ranking system. You can impact the Kingdom of God anywhere. Your ministry place is where you are at, right now. You are not a second-tier citizen in the Kingdom because you aren't a pastor or missionary, you are a child of the Most-High God, and you are on purpose for a purpose.

Consider a world where everyone is a pastor or missionary. Who would manufacture our cars or build our homes? Who would grow the food we eat or sew the clothes we wear? Our society needs all kinds of people with all kinds of talent. Each one of us has a unique calling. Your calling pairs up with the gifting that God placed in you when you were born. Your expertise puts you in a position of influence with people who may never meet a pastor or missionary.

For years, my mission field was the world of selling used cars. It is a messy dark place, but God put me there to be a light in a dark place and sell reliable transportation. If I hadn't been there, someone might have taken advantage of my customers. I wasn't in a pulpit, but my car ministry made a difference.

Now that you are close to retirement or in your retirement years, it's natural to think, "I finally have time to serve in my church." Serving in your church is great, but don't lose sight of the influence and talent you have. There are so many places that need you and your abilities. People need to know what you know. Your ministry spot is where God places you. It may not have four walls and a steeple, but it will have lost people who need directions to Jesus.

*The truth*: God called and ordained you as His missionary to everyone you meet. You are retired but not put out to pasture.

## Lie #4: The American Dream of retirement is biblical truth for Christians.

The American Dream of retirement is *not* biblical, and it's not guaranteed. It emphasizes material ownership, vacations, and living a life of leisure. The charade of the American Dream distracts us. When Christians live a life focused on pursuing the American Dream in their retirement, many miss God's best for their lives.

I have met many retired Christians who are more dedicated to improving their golf or tennis game than pursuing Jesus. What would our country look like if every retired Christian in America pursued Jesus instead of the American Dream? The American Dream distracts us from the ministry opportunities in our neighborhoods, on the golf league, the pickleball court, or wherever you spend your days. Spending your days investing in relationships with others always brings the best return.

Lie #4 is a sneaky lie. It sounds pleasant and innocuous. There is nothing wrong with having nice stuff, taking a vacation, or playing sports. The twist on the truth is, "At the end of my career, I can sit back, relax, stop working and be on vacation for the rest of my life. I will have peace, and life will be *good*." When we live that way, we waste our days and our talents. Jesus taught about this lie in the following parable.

Then he told them a story: "A rich man had a fertile farm that produced fine crops. He said to himself, 'What should I do? I don't have room for all my crops.' Then he said, 'I know! I'll tear down my barns and build bigger ones. Then I'll have room enough to store all my wheat and other goods. And I'll sit back and say to myself, "My friend, you have enough stored away for years to come. Now take it easy! Eat, drink, and be merry!"'

"But God said to him, 'You fool! You will die this very night. Then who will get everything you worked for?'

"Yes, a person is a fool to store up earthly wealth but not have a rich relationship with God." (Luke 12:16–21 NLT)

Jesus is saying that self-focused living is deceiving. We can be so focused on pleasure that we miss the essential. When we focus on pursuing the American Dream of Retirement, we miss the deep relationships God has for us, with Him and others. When leisure takes the place of leadership and influence, the next generation is left to figure things out for themselves. We can prevent that from happening.

*The truth*: Retirement is full of opportunities to build relationships for the Kingdom.

## How do these four lies impact our retirement?

Living under these four lies strangles our faith, but there is good news. Following Jesus is about a divine rescue plan for the rebellious children. Following Jesus is about bringing honesty, truth, hope, and love to a lost world. It's about selfless living. Following Jesus is about being transformed to be like Him. It's about grace and mercy. It's not about meeting in a building on Sundays; it's about setting the church loose on Sunday to bring healing on Monday through Saturday. Following Jesus isn't about you; it's all about Him. It is about realizing that no matter what we think we know about life, He knows better.

When these four lies infiltrate our retirement, we allow the enemy to decide where ministry takes place in our lives. These lies defeat the ultimate goal of retirement: freedom. In retirement, we have the freedom to try new things, meet new people, and go to new places. God uses that freedom to put us in front of people who need to meet Him. When we limit where we live out our faith, those around us miss the chance to meet Jesus.

*These lies defeat the ultimate goal of retirement: freedom.*

You don't have to live believing these lies. In the Name of Jesus, right now, I pray that the Lord will release you from the power of these lies in your life so you will experience true freedom in your retirement, forever. *Amen.*

## Ted Hains Shares a Story: Creative Enterprise Solving Economic Issues

I have a friend who is about 30 years my junior. Let's call him Jerry. We like to meet for lunch at the Waffle House near his work. Jerry and I share a love for our savior, Jesus Christ. I met Jerry in our church's life group, where most people are much younger than my wife and me. Jerry has a philosophy that "to be happy when you are old, do the things that you did or wanted to do when you were young."

Over the last couple of years, Jerry and I have been meeting on a random schedule. One of us will send a text, asking, "Are you free for lunch today?" We share a common military experience, and he had been a mechanic who could repair anything that came his way.

Only his wife and I had his complete trust to share the remarkably creative thing he had been doing for several years. He has a heart for older people with limited income and people with special needs. Jerry saw that these folks have only social security income, and it's hard to make ends meet. He realized their great need for affordable housing, so he put a plan together. Jerry decided to buy two-bedroom older brick houses that need some TLC. After making the necessary repairs, he then rents them for $300 a month per person, but it doesn't stop there.

Jerry gets very involved in the lives of the people in these homes by helping them with documents and paperwork, taking them to court appearances, and has even bailed some out of jail. Yet, he still has a full-time job. His wife is bilingual and helps with translation sometimes. He has often said, "If you're not willing to get fully involved in their lives, don't even try to do this."

Bottom Line: God gives each of us a unique set of gifts, talents, and abilities. He wants us to use them to minister to the least of these. Jerry found his niche— what's yours?

## Chapter 8 Questions

1. Take a look at the list of lies from this chapter. Is there a particular one that you could identify with believing? Write it here.

2. Knowing that the American Dream of retirement is a lie, how does that impact how you will move forward in your retirement years?

3. Ted hangs out with someone 30 years younger. What can you do to find someone like this in your life?

# 9

## iRetire4Him: Revealed

LIVING OUT YOUR FAITH with intentionality in your retirement is not a revolution; it's a revelation. Your work matters to God. Your retirement matters to God. Your life matters to God. How you spend your time with Him defines your very existence. He wants you to be purposeful and intentional with your living, right up until your last breath. You can be an ambassador to your generation.

There is purpose left in the life of every retiree you know. Whether they are active or homebound, they have something to give others, just like you.

> *Jesus came that we might have life and live it to the fullest—all the way to the end.*

Your friends who don't know Jesus are likely living a hopeless and hapless retirement. Some of them are wishing they could go back to work or get to the end of the game. They may pretend to be happy, but shortly after they retired, they realized that a lifelong vacation wasn't satisfying.

Jesus came that we might have life and live it to the fullest—all the way to the end. There is *so* much purpose left in your life. Invest your energy in the people God has placed around you.

Maybe you can start an "iRetire4Him" group to discuss how to live with intentionality, share ideas and stories, listen to iRetire4Him podcasts, and keep each other accountable. I imagine the Lord has been prompting you with names and ideas as you've been reading *iRetire4Him*. I can't wait to hear what He has inspired you to do with your retirement years. Please email me at jim@iWork4Him.com and tell me your story.

In the following chapters, I asked a few friends from ministries we have highlighted on the radio to write a letter of encouragement to you. These notes of encouragement will give you an idea of how you can put your faith into action in retirement by working with their ministry. I also included a letter from my retired mentor and an interview with a millennial asking for help from your generation. Don't miss this.

Martha and I invite you to find additional resources at www.iRetire4Him.com and sign the iRetire4Him covenant. It's free. I pray that you will commit to God to live out your every remaining day saying "iRetire4Him."

## Ted Hains Shares a Story: Looking Back

I just turned 88, and many years have passed since I gave my heart to Jesus. It has been my desire to serve Him since that day. There was always Christian music in my camera room, and Moody Radio played in my portrait prep rooms. I never once had any push back from a client. Our photography studio was sold in 1998, so I have been retired since then.

We already had a condo in Fort Myers, Florida, on a golf course, but that game was not for me. I had always loved things made of wood, so I joined the SW Woodturners and learned to make beautiful bowls, pens, and pepper mills. I turn this wood in my garage with the door open to engage the many walkers that often come up the driveway to see what I am doing. Sometimes they leave with a pocket testament in their hand. On one occasion, my neighbor, a retired English teacher, stopped to ask what I was doing.

"I'm making a bowl."

"Why? You can get one at Walmart for 59 cents."

"For the same reason, I go to the movie rather than read the book." When I finished the bowl, I gave it to her.

"Oh, thank you. It's beautiful."

I never know when a piece of wood, turned into a bowl, will touch a life and change a heart. I love what I do.

As I reflect on the past 88 years, I think about that rough timber on the log pile ready to be thrown into the fireplace. I like to work with maple, so I select a piece that is the proper size to turn. As I turn it on my lathe, a fantastic beauty begins to appear. Maple tends to display gorgeous patterns, and it is splatted (splatting is a decaying process that puts a line-connecting pattern throughout the wood.) Once this rough piece of wood is turned and sanded, I put on many layers of polyurethane. When applied, a masterpiece appears. Isn't that just like us in our Master's hands?

Each day as I awaken, I thank God for His mercy, do my devotions, and often put on the Full Armor of God through prayer. When I was 13, my pastor gave me Isaiah 40:31 as my life verse.

> But those who wait on the LORD shall renew *their* strength; They shall mount up with wings like eagles, they shall run and not be weary, they shall walk and not faint. (NKJV)

This verse described me as a young man, and it still defines me as an old man. I know God has a plan for my life, and He can use me until I hear Him say "Well done," as found in Matthew 25:21. He has a plan for you as well. Maybe it's iRetire4Him.

## Chapter 9 Questions

1. Who do you know that needs to be encouraged by reading this book? Please send them a copy today from www.iwork4him.com/bookstore.

2. What does it look like for you to be bold with your retired Christian friends and challenge them to step up to an iRetire4Him lifestyle?

3. Ted closes out this book by looking back on his life with fondness and looking forward with anticipation. When you do the same, how does Jesus fit in going forward?

# Part II

## Faith and Work Ministry Collaborators

PERSONAL NOTES ARE SPECIAL and rare these days. The following pages are a collection of special notes from friends who love to work with Christ-following retirees in their ministries, friends whose ministries are focused explicitly on discipling retirees, and even a message from my current mentor, who is a perfect example of someone living out iRetire4Him.

Outreach Magazine shared their recent interview of Grant Skeldon and his book, *The Passion Generation*. It is the cry from the millennial generation to you, the retired generations.

These notes are written to you by friends and colaborers in the Kingdom of God. We honor them in this collaborative effort because the Kingdom is about The One.

Enjoy.

# 10

## Note from Bruce Bruinsma

### The Retirement Reformation

YOU ARE CALLED TO BE faithful for a lifetime.

Isn't it strange that we are sidelined by the siren call to "leisure" during our time of greatest maturity, understanding, and potential life impact? We have succumbed to the world's view of what they call retirement. It's sold as one homogeneous period, highlighted by physical and mental decline, with the associated goal of jamming as much leisure into the time that's left. This definition is both depressing and wrong. As Christians, we have something more and something better in our future.

I was sitting with a friend of mine, John, in a local eatery. He invested the better part of 30 years leading a local ministry. At 67, he is handing the reins to a younger associate. As we began talking, I noticed he looked and sounded relieved. I asked him about the transition. He shared about the weight being lifted from his shoulders and how he was looking forward to traveling with his wife of 40 years. After congratulating him, I asked, "So what are you going to do next?" His look reminded me of the proverbial deer in headlights.

"You know," he said, "I haven't really thought about it. I'm sure something will turn up."

John was quite clear about what he was retiring from and clueless about what he was retiring to. During the next 30 minutes, I introduced him to the reality of longevity: "John, it's 30 years. The odds are that 30 years is the length of time ahead of you." Even his deer in headlights look glazed over. "Seriously?"

Then I asked him how he connected with his ministry. He told me the story of the clear calling he had to serve and to serve with that ministry. It was a touching story of his being uniquely called and specially prepared for the responsibility. "So," I asked him, "has God stopped calling you now?"

He looked confused and said, "What do you mean?"

"If He prepared you for your last 30 years of ministry, don't you think he's prepared you for another 30? It might look different, but we are all called to be faithful for a lifetime."

John and I met a few weeks later. He'd accessed the RetirementReformation.org website and downloaded all three of my books in the Future Funded Ministry series. He doesn't like to spend money, and they were free. *Finding Freedom*, *Moving Forward*, and the latest one, *Charting your Course*, all helped, notably *Charting your Course*. He then connected with the heart of the Retirement Reformation by purchasing my book by that name. In the Retirement Reformation book, I talk about the issues faced in retirement other than money. The book is available wherever books are sold online.

The glazed look is now gone, and there is certainly no deer in his headlights. He was just excited. He was excited to realize that God was nowhere near done with him yet. He realized that the last 67 years were only the prelude to what was ahead. Then he paused and asked, "Should I feel guilty taking the trips we've planned?" Of course not. Remember this: leisure, rest, and rejuvenation are important, while your future role in ministry is critical. No one can honestly defend 30 years of golf or travel; however, 20–30% of your time focusing on yourself and your family is perfectly reasonable. Take a year's sabbatical, and then embrace what has lasting meaning and purpose. You won't regret it, and you will even live longer.

I've shared John's story because it reflects the status quo of so many. John was entering the initial stage of retirement. It is interesting to note that there are three stages of retirement. Each stage has its unique properties and requires a reexamination of who you are, what God is calling you to do during the next season, and a clear understanding of why you are doing it.

As I move into my late 70s, I've never been more passionate or had so much energy and as many ideas as I have now. This passion and the energy it generates comes because God has called me to the Retirement Reformation message. I'm passionate and energized, realizing that I'm part of the generations with the potential to impact God's Kingdom in ways we cannot even imagine. Challenging and encouraging those empty nesters or those who did not have children and are approaching their 50s, 60s, 70s, 80s, and yes, beyond, to engage in the invigorating journey to discover your big *why*? *Why* are you here? Where are you going? What is your unique role in the Kingdom going forward? You are not forgotten. You are equipped. You are not to be ignored; you are to be valued. You are not to be set aside; you are to be engaged. Listen to what Jesus said in John 15:16: "You did not choose me, but I chose you and appointed you so that you might go and bear fruit—fruit that will last..." (NIV)

Jesus did not just throw out useless or irrelevant platitudes or high-sounding rhetoric. He meant every word. You have been called and have been given margin (time), capacity, and capital. These are the necessary ingredients to respond to His unique call for the rest of your life. Yes, we are all to love our neighbors. I'm convinced that God has a unique way for you to show that love. And when you do, you will begin to experience those wonderful fruits of the Spirit: love, joy, peace, patience, kindness, gentleness, and self-control. Who better to trust with the keys to the Kingdom?

So, what's next? Maybe this is the 11th commandment for our time: get connected and figure out your *why*. Discover who you are, who you have become, listen to the promptings of the Holy Spirit, find your direction, and get started. The fields are white unto harvest. Your job is to represent Jesus in all the unique ways He has prepared for you.

The Retirement Reformation exists to start and encourage a new movement. A movement of God among those approaching retirement age and way beyond. There are 30,000,000 of us. If only 10,000,000 find their *why*, listen to the Spirit's direction, and got moving, we'd change our country and perhaps the world. Many are praying for revival. We need a revival of the most capable, experienced, and insightful people of our time, you and me.

On the Retirement Reformation website, you will find several pathways to finding your *why*. You will also find roads that lead to *action*. Read my book, access the prayer guide, read the devotions, take the eight-week small group study (it can be done on your own), read Bergstrom's book *The Third Calling*, or go to their website and connect with their material. There are many resources for you. My challenge to you is to do something leading to understanding your *why* and then discover your passion. Next, join a growing and active group of Jesus followers and impact your part of the world with love in action. Your retirement *why* could be as close as your work associates or the neighbors around your block. Whatever it is, get busy. You'll never be happier. And don't forget there may be another 30 years ahead. We are each called to be faithful for a lifetime.

**Bruce Bruinsma**
*www.RetirementReformation.org*
*Bruce@RetirementReformation.org*

Champion of the Retirement Reformation and Co-Host of the iRetire4Him Podcast with Jim Brangenberg

**iWork4Him Show**

- http://bit.ly/39b1n8K

# 11

## Note from Doug Fagerstrom

*Marketplace Chaplains*

MANY OF OUR MARKETPLACE Chaplains are retired men and women. Each chaplain is a mature, godly person who loves Jesus, rightly handles biblical truth, and is passionate about pointing people to Jesus Christ. Meet a few of our retired servants.

Chaplain Donna called me one day to share a remarkable story. Four weeks earlier, she had the joy of leading an employee to Jesus. The person asked, "Donna, what do I do now?" Chaplain Donna's response was to find a local church and begin growing in her new life in Christ. Donna provided some good choices, and the employee found a church. As the chaplain shared with me this incredible journey, she then said, "I just got a call from the employee inviting me to her church. Her entire family started attending church, and they are all getting baptized." I just had to share my joy!

Henry is retired from a Fortune 500 company as the former HR director. As a chaplain, his care for people, combined with his relationship with Jesus and knowledge of the Scriptures, makes Henry a confidant with every employee. One day, I shadowed Henry in a manufacturing plant. An employee saw us and immediately ran to Chaplain Henry, gave him a bearhug, and yelled, "Thanks, Chap." A bit surprised and almost embarrassed, Henry responded, "Thanks for what?" The man reminded the chaplain how they had discussed the employee's difficult marriage, and Henry encouraged him to go home and be kind to his wife. The employee had grown up his entire life, never seeing kindness in marriage, much less encouraged to exercise the simple virtue. The employee then said, "Chaplain, it really works." After some laughter and a time of prayer, we parted. It was weeks later that the employee came to Christ through Henry's witness and extra kindness.

About a year ago, I visited a young man who was in his mid-twenties. The young employee shared how retired chaplain Clois, sixty years his senior, had been discipling him over the past couple of years. He showed me long text messages of spiritual encouragement, Bible verses, and written prayers from the senior chaplain. Clois demonstrates how age is not a relational barrier, overcome by authentic love, care, and genuine interest in seeing people of all ages grow closer to Jesus. Clois breaks the norms. But so do all our chaplains.

Chaplain Bob was a pastor for over 45 years. After he retired, he was restless and did not know what to do next in his lifelong commitment to serve Jesus. A friend called him and invited him to join the team at Marketplace Chaplains. His first comment to me when we spent time together was simply, "I have never loved a role in ministry like this." He exclaimed that he had so much freedom and opportunity to build relationships with non-churched people like never before. He could visit, pray with people, listen to amazing stories, and point people to hope and help through Jesus. He went on: "I get to love people at a funeral, perform weddings, and even get to lead a worship service at a veterans retirement center." Bob's joy is contagious. I would say he is not getting old, maybe younger and full of life!

I love our older chaplains. They bring great balance to our chaplain teams with a tremendous diversity of age, gender, and ethnic heritages. Team members love and respect all the chaplains, yet look to the mature chaplains for wisdom in life and ministry. The door is wide open for more people of all ages. Retired? Contact us. We would love to share how God still has a marvelous place for you. You are not finished. Neither is God!

*Thanks, Doug. Readers, there is a huge need for you to get involved in the unique and powerful ministry of chaplaincy in the workplace. Marketplace Chaplains is one organization you should check out. Your years of experience and wisdom make you uniquely qualified to invest your life in others. While not everyone is a perfect fit for workplace chaplaincy, you will never know until you give them a call.*

*—Jim Brangenberg, iWork4Him*

**Doug Fagerstrom**
*www.mchapusa.com*

President and CEO,
Marketplace Chaplains

Marketplace Chaplains was founded in 1984 and now serves over one million employees and family members in over 1,015 companies and 4,000+ locations in all 50 states plus Canada and Mexico. 1,700+ chaplains serve companies in many industries, including a strategic emphasis on senior living communities caring for staff, residents, and family members.

**iWork4Him Show**

- http://bit.ly/2Xid3ks

# 12

## Note from Jeff Brown

*Corporate Chaplains*

WHAT ARE CORPORATE chaplains? We are caregivers in the workplace. Employees in companies across America are dealing with challenging situations in their lives, bringing pain to work. Not only are they hurting, but their issues affect their work and the people around them. The average company owner feels like his/her hands are tied and simply doesn't know how to help. The chaplains bring skilled help and encouragement that brings changed lives and enhances company culture.

On average, working people spend 90,000 hours of their lives at work. The issues they face around children at home, technology, health matters, and areas like distributed workforce are complex and increasing. People need hope and encouragement, and when they don't find it, their performance at work, attendance, and longevity suffers.

According to a recent survey done in 2019, very few Americans consistently attend church.[1] They have marginal relationships with neighbors as found in a Pew Research study,[2] and families are often dispersed. HR professionals have strict guidelines, supervisors are not equipped, and owners feel restricted. "Chaplaincy allows me to care for my employees like my heart wants to but my title does not allow," said Mike Emerson, the CEO of Huntington Steel. Chaplains show up daily and ask, "How can I care for the employees today?"

The term "chaplain" comes from the Latin word *cappella* for a cloak. The name Chaplain grew out of the story of St. Martin meeting a man begging in the rain with no cloak. He chose to tear his cloak in two and share the support with the man instead of giving him the whole cloak. Today, chaplains offer support in much the same way through sharing the burden. (Cambridge University Hospitals, www.cuh.nhs.uk/chaplaincy/history-chaplaincy)

Our chaplains help more than just the employees who are going through challenging situations. Our businesses and organizations that we serve tell us they see happier staff, better work rates, and encouraging growth. It's our passion to serve employees and see all levels of the organization gain from our ministry.

Many of our chaplains are young and getting started in a full career of caregiving. However, we also have many retired ministers who have a heart to "lay up treasures in Heaven" and don't want to retire by the poolside. What better way to make a difference as a part-time or full-time chaplain even in your golden years? Your experience, savvy, wisdom, and love for the Gospel need an outlet, and the workplace may be the perfect fit.

Founded in 1996 as a 501(c)(3) non-profit, Corporate Chaplains of America is the largest full-time workplace chaplaincy organization in America. Today, we serve over 360,000 people (employees, spouses, and families) in almost every state across the country. "People have full-time problems, and I want my chaplain to have a full-time mindset," said Peter Freissle, owner of Polydeck Screen Corp.

*Story:* When an employee sees another employee die at work, it changes them. A few years ago, I was a chaplain at a company where a fork truck driver just died on his vehicle. The leadership team called me in because they simply did not know what to do. I was dispatched to the home for notification, spent days talking with shocked fellow-workers (hearing of their account and other old memories of death), and then performing a memorial service at the worksite to help bring closure. If properly handled, these events can be culture changers for good even in a time of crisis.

## Questions We Often Hear

*Is that legal?*

Absolutely! The program works because of three cornerstones: it is voluntary, permission-based, and confidential. Employees can opt-in or out of the program based on their choice. Also, the chaplain always asks for permission before providing any services. Finally, everything the chaplain learns from an employee is strictly confidential (legal requirements demand that someone expressing a desire to hurt themselves or someone else being the only exceptions). Employees quickly realize they can trust the chaplain, and as the employee, they determine the level and degree of care they receive from their chaplain. CCA is a Christian agency that focuses on sharing truth while supporting all faith backgrounds.

## How does it work?

Chaplains provide weekly contact with employees through on-site rounds. During these visits, the chaplain briefly interacts with the employee just as a friend would. Over time, friendships and trust develop. We have found that when people are going through a tough time in life, they would prefer to turn to a friend than a total stranger. Because crisis doesn't always occur from 9–5, the chaplain is on call through a pager system 24/7. People need to understand there is still someone on the other end of the line, ready to help.

Chaplains also provide pro-active engagement with distributed workforces through weekly points of encouragement and resources on our *My Chaplain* app and other forms of media. They work together with a nationwide network of full-time chaplains who can respond to distant situations.

Types of issues we address:

- Discouragement and pain
- Stress
- Financial concerns
- Family issues
- Workplace morale
- Conflict
- Addictions
- Suicide

- Domestic disputes
- Hospital visits
- Serious illness
- Death and dying
- Grief care

*How would I get my company started with a chaplain?*

Typically, an owner who wants to do more for their employees (a desire to lay up treasures in Heaven) will hear about the concept. They would be visited by a member of our field development team to listen to a brief overview of the program. Since we don't have contracts but instead operate under a letter of intent, companies have the option to opt-out at any time. Upon acceptance, the company would agree to pay for the services per employee per month. This rate is extremely low compared to other employee benefits they are already providing.

The process of introducing chaplains to your company is simple. First, an all-employee orientation is set up. The primary purpose of this light-hearted, 12-minute presentation is to calm the perceived fears of all employees about the idea of having a chaplain. Next, the chaplain starts to make weekly rounds. This weekly visit is a short 30-second to three-minute moment of encouragement for each employee every week. In those weekly conversations, employees will start to engage with the chaplain at a deeper level. This is where chaplains provide what we call care sessions. Finally, in complicated or long-distance situations, the chaplain will secure assistance from our nationwide network of chaplains to assist as needed.

*What qualifies this person to be my Chaplain?*

Our chaplains are genuinely called to this profession. They have a deep-seated love for people as followers of Christ. For CCA, this typically means a full-time career where the chaplain can be focused and single-minded in their work. Our chaplains are all expected to be seminary-trained and ordained. It is essential that all our chaplains have seven to ten years of workplace experience. Understanding how to punch a time clock and recognizing the importance of profits, productivity, and the pressures of the modern business world help make our chaplains better caregivers and benefit the company's bottom line. Finally, our recruits go through a multi-stage, rigorous interview process to ensure we are providing the best possible chaplain to care for these very precious employees. *Our chaplains come from diverse backgrounds and age ranges.*

Retaining quality, healthy employees in our day can be challenging. An intentional, decisive plan to care for these valuable assets with mind, body, and soul care is not only good business but, more importantly, builds a culture and leaves a legacy that really matters.

See chaplain.org for more information and other great stories!

*Thanks, Jeff. Reader, there is such a huge need for you to get involved in the unique and powerful ministry of chaplaincy in the workplace. Corporate Chaplains is one organization you should check out. Your years of experience and wisdom make you uniquely qualified to invest your life in others. While not everyone is a perfect fit for workplace chaplaincy, you will never know until you give them a call.*

—*Jim Brangenberg, iWork4Him*

**Jeff Brown**
*www.chaplain.org*

VP, Quality & Strategic Initiatives
at Corporate Chaplains of America

**iWork4Him Show**

- http://bit.ly/2Xid3ks

---

[1] www.statista.com/statistics/245491/church-attendance-of-americans/

[2] www.pewresearch.org/fact-tank/2019/08/15/facts-about-neighbors-in-u-s/

# 13

## Note from Rich Timmons

*Pocket Testament League*

AFTER MY WIFE AND I sold our business, we found ourselves asking the big question: so, now what? We still make it a practice to carry our Gospels of John with us wherever we go, as we had done throughout our marketing career. But now we became more intentional by selecting particular Gospel covers. We were praying the covers we chose would match up with the person we would meet that day. For example, when we stop for breakfast or lunch, I always have the Rose Gospel ready to leave with a nice tip for our waitress. Then I stop at the local gun shop. I always have my patriotic Gospel with me, hoping to share it with a fellow patriot.

The next discussion we had was with our pastor. He knew for a long time that I was a PTL board member. We wanted to do more than hand out Gospels individually. We wanted to motivate others to embrace the PTL motto, "Read, Carry, Share," which came from the lips of PTL founder, Helen Cadbury, more than 125 years ago. It was successful then and is successful now because God's Word is the same then as it is now. We believe that if someone we hand a Gospel of John to will take the time to read it with an open heart and mind, God does the work of drawing them closer to that incredible, magnificent moment when someone's empty heart begins to fill up with joy, peace, and love. They begin to understand that when Jesus died, the most brutal death on the cross that anyone could imagine, He did it to save that new reader/new believer.

PTL has many, many stories about how someone was handed a Gospel of John, and in a most unusual way, God, Himself, used that little booklet, the Gospel of John, to bring someone to salvation. What a blessing! How exciting!

My pastor encouraged me to share with every group within our church why we *must* somehow, someway, share our faith with family, neighbors, and strangers.

We did that.

One day I got a call from John, my pastor. He said, "I want you to preach on Sunday. I want you to share your testimony. I want you to share the PTL story, and I want you to teach everyone how easy it is to share the Gospel of John. Oh, and you have 45 minutes." Of course, just like Pastor John, I ran overtime.

We had two long tables with many different Gospel covers—something for everyone. We had boxes and boxes of Gospels under the tables. We were ready. After preaching two services, we had 348 people sign up and commit to sharing the Gospel of John, and approximately 5,100 Gospels left the church that day, and the numbers continue to grow.

Since then, we have spoken at several other local churches. We share with other pastors the joy and fulfillment of those who have signed up committing to share a Gospel when they get that "poke" from the Lord.

This simple note from a 24-year-old man may inspire you to join me as a member at www.PTL.org.

> Hey Rich, I just wanted to share a little "poke" that I had earlier today when I was coming out of a hardware store. This older woman, maybe 65, had just finished paying and was walking out behind me. I held the door for her, and we made some small talk about the weather and some construction in the area when I felt a little poke from the Lord. I happened to pick the rose-themed Gospel when I left my house earlier. So, I said, "Quick question for you: when's the last time a young man gave you a rose?"
>
> She stopped and thought about it for a few seconds and said with a smile, "I'm getting up there in age, ya know, so I think it's been quite a few years now!" I reached into my pocket for the Gospel and then handed it to her. "Well, this is for you." She sort of giggled and said thank you as we both got into our cars.
>
> It felt so natural and sweet; I long for more interactions like that. Thanks for the Gospels and the pickup line!

Sharing a Gospel with someone is the missing ingredient in our lives. (John 15:11) When we share, we experience the joy and peace that only God can give us. It is the most satisfying experience that words cannot explain.

**Rich Timmons**

Board Member, The Pocket Testament League

Rich founded and led a marketing communications firm for 45 years, which he has since sold. He was saved by the grace of God 43 years ago. He has been married to Julie for more than 50 years, with three children plus an adult foster son. His passion is sharing the Gospel as often as he can.

### iWork4Him Shows with Pocket Testament League

- http://bit.ly/38oIJer
- http://bit.ly/35mSjwj

# 14

## Note from Danita Bye

### *Millennials Matter*

LEADERS BUILD LEADERS.

Most experienced business owners focus on high growth and performance. Yes, business results are important. Many leaders, however, know what matters even more—the legacy they leave at work and at home. This legacy is the mark of true wisdom and effective stewardship.

We live in the wealthiest world during the wealthiest time in history. And some of us even live in the wealthiest state or suburb. In Luke 12:48, Jesus said that to whom much is given, much will be required. We have been given much, haven't we? Often, what we've been given goes beyond what we imagined when we were young, planning our careers and crafting our life goals.

What do Jesus's words mean today?

Mentoring the next generation is part of what is required of wise leaders. Millennials are entering a global economy filled with threats and opportunities that previous generations would struggle even to imagine. Robotics, artificial intelligence, quantum mechanics, and genetic engineering have left us grappling with complex, far-reaching issues. Understandably, next-gen leaders are filled with mixed emotions, ranging from fear to excitement, about making a positive difference.

The world is crazy. Young leaders need guidance. They need us to pass on the wisdom we have gained through experience. In turn, we need fresh insight into how God wants us to mentor and coach this generation to help maximize their influence in the global community.

Your legacy-making doesn't end when you retire. In *The Making of a Leader: Recognizing the Lessons and Stages of Leadership Development*, Robert Clinton spotlights five phases of leadership development. What he found in his studies of leaders is that many stop at phase four. They've built successful businesses and are looking forward to retirement when they can kick back and take it easy. That is what they've been working toward their whole life.

But Clinton proposes that *every preceding phase in our lives is actually part of our preparation for stage five, which often emerges after retirement.* Every seemingly unrelated event we experience—the people we meet, and the work we do—they're all part of God's preparation to lead us to this next stage. Clinton calls it *convergence.*

Stage five is when we can have the broadest impact. Millennials need us senior leaders of proven moral character to impart wisdom, so they get the leadership traction needed to lead well in this rapidly changing culture.

Now is not the time for us to rest. It's the time for us to rise up as mentors and coaches. Regardless of our ages—and regardless of whether or not we have formal or informal mentoring, coaching, or managing roles in our companies. Leading and serving are incalculable gifts we can give to those who will continue blazing trails where we leave off.

It's time for character-based business leaders to live out the truth of our calling regarding the plan, place, and position of our collective impact on the world. We have the high responsibility and urgent calling to mentor millennials so they can tap their vast potential. I believe they have the capacity to be the greatest generation yet.

What seemingly unrelated, disconnected events have happened over the course of *your* life to date? Perhaps like me, you've become aware that God is now merging all your past experiences, talents, skills, and wisdom for a greater purpose.

This is our legacy, the moment that reveals the culmination of all we have learned. It's our calling to build wise, well-grounded leaders of character and virtue.

You are being called to make a difference and to build next-gen leaders. More specifically, you have the responsibility to coach and mentor your next-gen leader, the one who comes to mind as you are reading. If you've ever watched a relay race, you know how important it is to pass on the baton to the next runner. Will you accept the challenge to mentor, coach, and disciple up-and-coming leaders?

We must not abdicate this responsibility, and there is great reward in embracing the opportunity. Be proactive and strategic. It's time.

Perhaps you're reaching for the mentoring baton, considering its weight, but you're not quite certain of your footing, where to focus, or where to go. Maybe you're thinking, *No one's going to listen to me anyway.*

I wrote the following poem, "The Calling," during a time when I needed strengthening for the journey. In sharing this poem with you, it is my wholehearted prayer that its words confirm your calling—that you use your uniquely crafted talents to make a difference in the lives of the millennials within your sphere of influence.

### The Calling

I am calling you,
I am anointing you,
I am setting you apart for a divine purpose.
Rise up and walk in it.
Turn your back on how you've done it before.
Behold, I am making all things new.[1]
I am opening new vistas and opportunities.

Walk in confidence.

Excerpt from *Millennials Matter: Proven Strategies for Building Your Next-Gen Leader,* 2019. All rights reserved.

## Danita Bye, M.A.
*www.DanitaBye.com*

Danita is an executive leadership coach and author of *Millennials Matter: Proven Strategies for Building Your Next-Gen*. She's served as Forbes Coaches Council contributor, Harvard Business School MBA sales coach, Board of Trustees for several Christian universities, and as a TEDx speaker on Millennial leadership.

### iWork4Him Show

- http://bit.ly/3hWTlEj

---

[1] Revelation 21:5 ESV

# 15

## Note from Bob Spence

*Jim Brangenberg's Mentor*

AS I SIT HERE AND write this, I am a 73-year-old man who moved to Florida when he was 70 with the intention to, at the very least, semi-retire. Then, why am I now still working close to full-time? I continue to work because I enjoy my work, and I can continue to share Jesus with so many people! It all gives my life a sense of purpose.

As a Christian, how am I to view retirement? Am I to retreat to the couch? Am I to spend day after day in recreational activities? Am I to devote a lot of time to see how many restaurants I can visit? If we retire from our work life, do we also retire from doing God's work? Retirement is not in the Bible. Does that mean God expects us to keep working until He calls us home? No. However, He expects us to keep a Kingdom focus, continue to stay close to Him, and continue to share the Word with others. He wants us to have a clear sense of purpose even though we are not actively engaged in the marketplace.

I live in a community for those 55 and over in Florida. It is estimated that at least 80% of my neighbors are fully retired. Some do volunteer work in a church or for a charity or contribute time to a local school reading to elementary children. They obviously have maintained a sense of purpose. Others play golf and/or spend time at the community clubhouse involved in various interest clubs and/or playing cards. I guess they have a sense of purpose, but is it Kingdom-based?

If I chose to stop working as a consultant, I have no doubt what I would determine to do. I would devote more time and energy to my Christian artwork. I would devote more time and energy to my work in men's ministry activities and other ways to serve at church. I would volunteer at a local school and read to young children. I would be busy, which reminds me of my father, who retired from an engineering position after 43 years with the same company.

I remember several years ago asking my father how he liked retirement. He told me that he was busier retired than when he worked. And he added that he no longer had any paid holidays or vacation. Why was he so busy? Because he had volunteer work at the church and his woodworking hobby in his basement. He maintained a sense of purpose.

It amazes me how some view retirement. To some retirees, the world owes them. In their thinking, they worked hard all those years and are entitled to a peaceful and restful retirement. Here is what I often witness living in a 55-and-over community. The retiree spends a lot of time playing games, cards, or golf. They go to a whole lot of restaurants. They periodically attend church on Sunday. They complain a lot about aches and pains. They like to go to HOA meetings and complain. I feel sorry for them.

What if they rejoiced for each additional day the Lord gives them? What if they spent time in the Word? What if they took advantage of many volunteer activities? What if they went beyond Sunday services and attended Bible study programs? What if they spent some time clarifying their purpose as a retiree?

What is retirement really? It is, simply stated, a job change. You no longer need to report to a job in the marketplace. You now have time to be in the marketplace walking and talking like Jesus. You now have time to truly serve others. It is a time to serve and focus on others. Retirement is not all about you. It is all about serving the Lord by helping others. Get off the couch and get out in the marketplace as a witness for the Lord!

So, what about you? When I interview leaders and managers, I always ask them this question: what is your driving purpose? I get a whole range of responses and sometimes a blank stare. My driving purpose has not changed. My purpose is to be a servant leader, to as much as humanly possible, walk and talk like Jesus. And this purpose does not waver or change through the years and even into retirement. Every day is a blessing to behold and to love the Lord and share this love with others. *What is your driving purpose? How are you fulfilling it?*

## Bob Spence

Coach, Trainer, Leader

In 1987, after a 20-year career in education, Bob founded an HR firm in San Diego, CA, to provide human resource services to clients whose primary focus was on hiring the right fit and match for their client's companies. Through these years, Bob has completed more than 300 key leader searches and has trained hundreds of managers using his trademarked Choosing Winners™ system.

Bob is now based in Davenport, Florida. In 2016, he received the HR Lifetime Achievement Award from Columbus CEO Magazine. Bob is a men's ministry leader and also a Christian abstract artist in Davenport, Florida.

### iWork4Him Show

- http://bit.ly/396Z6LI

# 16

---

# Interview with Noted
# Millennial Grant Skeldon

---

*Speaking to Christ-Following Retirees*

*This interview was featured as the cover article in the December 2019 issue of Outreach Magazine and shared with permission.*

*Interviewee: Grant Skeldon – Author, Speaker, and President of www.InitiativeNetwork.org*

*Interview by Paul J. Pastor[1] Editor at Large, Outreach Magazine*

## Generation Underchallenged

Millennials haven't rejected church because it's too exclusive or too traditional. That's what you'll hear on TV or read in blogs. But it's not true…. Millennials have rejected the church for a pretty simple reason: the church has asked too little of them….

The church has failed to call millennials out of their ordinary lives and into the extraordinary life of Jesus. The church has failed to invite millennials into a great commission. Instead, we've settled for just a decent commission....

Why is the most cause-oriented generation in the world neglecting the most cause-oriented organization in the world: the church? Because we have taken the greatest cause ever and watered it down to attending an event. Merely showing up on Sunday and inviting all your friends is just not that compelling. We have a generation that's basically saying, "Send me; I'll go." And we're replying, "No. Wait. Stay here." (Grant Skeldon, *The Passion Generation*)

Grant Skeldon is the founder of The Initiative Network, an organization empowering members of the millennial generation to serve in the city of Dallas. In his book *The Passion Generation: The Seemingly Reckless, Definitely Disruptive, But Far From Hopeless Millennials* (Zondervan), Skeldon outlines a path to engaging younger generations that balances fresh insights into generational dynamics with a very old solution—rediscovering the relevance of the Great Commission plan to make disciples in a world where deep and generative relationships can seem in short supply.

*Outreach* caught up with Skeldon to discuss the conundrums and contributions of an unfairly maligned generation, and to ask how churches can help unleash the energy of the passion generation for the cause of Jesus.

Q. Your book's been out for about a year now, and you've been speaking widely. Tell me about the response that's come from people working to understand the millennial generation?

A. The response has really been wonderful. People know this conversation needs to happen. Most of the readers have been pastors, parents, or employers. Each in their own way is trying to figure out how to retain and engage this generation. As a side note—to illustrate the idea of retention—I recently heard a statistic that the average millennial will have had 14 jobs by the age of 40. This is more than just restlessness, of course, but there is this rising trend of mobility—job to job, city to city, church to church. Millennials "switch ladders" like crazy.

The book has gotten great responses from groups like moms or young adult pastors. So many people are looking for a chance to understand and engage the younger adults around them. The need is huge. While the groups who have welcomed the book are diverse, I definitely had the pastor in mind when I wrote it.

Q. What was your goal in writing?

A. To shift the culture of the church in how we relate to my generation. To change the church's scorecard.

Q. Scorecard?

A. Yeah, what we measure. To reach millennials, I believe we must prioritize discipleship as a part of our scorecard. Many churches have been serious about measur-

ing attendance or giving. Great. Why don't we have
the same care in measuring how many people are discipling other people? Sure, it's kind of hard, but it's also central. As I say in the book, I don't think churches
have a millennial problem. I think churches have a discipleship problem. My joke (pardon me in advance) is
what if we simply made the commission great again?

This generation is dying to be a part of something
bigger than they are. Unfortunately, the world sometimes gives young adults bigger responsibilities than
the church does. The church has lost the message of
"Come, follow me," replacing it with … what? "Come,
and listen to me"?

That posture has lost us many strong assets in the
next generation.

Q. How has the response been to that message?

A. Well, it's not like they don't know it, in theory. But it's
still been convicting for many, I think. They feel
they've missed this. But it also brings energy and hope.
Many pastors are kind of tired of basically just being
event planners. This can be a breath of fresh air.

Pastors with impact, in my experience, had significant mentor figures when they were young. Someone
older invested in them—believed in them, and connected them to others, and allowed them to fail safely.
They recognize the importance of discipleship in their
own journey. They know they wouldn't be who they
are today if you removed their key mentors.

Q. That dynamic is powerful and true of every generation.
We've been wrestling with discipleship for 20 centu-

ries, right? Tell me more about what is specific to what you call "the millennial problem."

A. To many churches today millennials feel like a problem. Their lack of attendance, let alone membership. Their lack of giving. One thing I often get on my generation for is a lack of honor toward those who are older than they are. Often when I speak to groups, pastors will come up and express that they'd love to mentor younger people—but none are asking them.

My generation needs to show up more, I think— and be willing to stay when things get tough. Many pastors observe that young people don't stay through a problem; they'll just leave and never even tell you why. Often pastors are not sure exactly what they're doing or not doing that's causing that. Often, it's a bit of a pain point for them. In this way, investing in discipleship is a bit of a chicken-and-egg situation. Millennials might not stay if you don't invest, but how can you invest if they don't stay?

I try to encourage pastors to be more proactive in their jobs. My generation is likely not going to seek you out. So, we need you to be like Jesus and engage us. Be proactive. And remember that when discipleship is hard it means that you're in good company. It was difficult for Jesus too.

In the end, you must have realistic expectations. There isn't a silver bullet of discipleship.

Q. Talk to me about the challenges facing intergenerational discipleship.

A. Well, younger people tend to only hang out with younger people who look like they do, are in a similar stage of life, and so forth. That habit runs deep. It's a big challenge, honestly.

The greatest commodity of the next generation is free time. But we waste a lot of it. Not necessarily in sinful things—it just goes away. A lot of young passionate Christians want to be a part of something bigger than they are. It's important to bond with your peers, but if that's all we have, we're like seventh graders asking other seventh graders for dating advice. We are just doing what's right in our eyes, like that line from the book of Judges. But we can learn from someone who's 10 or 20 years ahead of us.

One of the biggest issues with intergenerational unity, though, comes from the older generation. There's such a culture in the church of making fun of the next generation—dismissing them, demeaning them. It's as bad as the culture in the world, or worse. I don't know if there's a group in America that the church can make fun of more—and you almost get applauded for it. Nobody wants to be a part of a group with a culture of making fun of you. It's dishonorable. So, when that comes into play—all the little jokes and snide remarks—I don't know why we are shocked that young people don't want to go to churches that have that kind of culture.

Q. As I was reading your book, the word "reconciliation" came to mind. Generational resentment is mutual. A young man I know recently said, "It's like the boomers borrowed the car of America with a full tank and brought it back dented and empty." Across nearly every metric, boomers enjoyed unprecedented entitlement and security—yet they blame those younger than they are for "disrupting" deeply broken systems. With much of this simmering under the surface, don't we have to speak to some hard truths to really move forward effectively between generations?

A. Yes. Behind the scenes, I've begun to lead small retreats of radically diverse young Christian leaders in their 20s or 30s. I have an affinity for young Christians working in culture and influencing culture. We often talk about reconciliation in terms of race, but it applies to generations too. When that happens it's usually because of shared experiences.

It all comes down to relationship. If you really want reconciliation, you need to have empathy and compassion for people who don't look like you. Have dinner. Get to know their family. Invite them over. Slow down with them for a minute. Really talk.

Q. Fair enough. What are some of our biggest excuses for neglecting discipleship?

A. From older generations, "I don't have time" or "I don't feel qualified" or "I'm afraid I'm not living a life that I'm proud of a younger person seeing." In that sense, discipleship is great accountability for older generations.

From younger generations? Busyness. The young person has to be hungry enough for this relationship to prioritize it and move their life around to fit the older person's schedule.

— 137 —

Q. What do you say to an older person who just feels like they can't fit discipleship into their schedule?

A. If you're really saying to someone, "Come, follow me," then you're not adding another event to your calendar. You're including someone in your calendar. That's discipleship.

Q. What are millennials looking for in a mentor?

A. Often, a parent figure or an older person in a healthy marriage. We are a generation hugely impacted by the divorces of boomers. Authenticity, as well. People in my generation are extremely attracted to figures like Francis Chan and Bob Goff or Beth Moore. It's not because of the speaking or events or books. It's about being honest and raw and real. We think, "Man I want to live like that when I get older. What is that going to require of me today?"

Sometimes, too, it's specific mentorship in a skill or craft that they want to practice. Many of us haven't found our careers yet or are still growing in them.

Q. What's one myth many older Christians have about connecting with younger believers?

A. That they must be "relatable"—hip or cool or relevant. The worst thing you can do is to get a tattoo or skinny jeans or a cooler worship band to try and connect. This generation has been marketed at by older people their whole lives. They are really good at sniffing out when someone isn't genuine.

Don't look for tips and tricks. There's no shortcut for how to reach the next generation. Our job isn't to be relevant; our job is to make disciples. Those disciples will be more relevant than we could ever be.

Q. Many of the problems we face today are really problems of the status quo—whether they're economic, environmental, religious, or political. How does a young person know when to ignore the advice of older generations—perhaps because it got us into this mess? How do we glean wisdom without internalizing their mistakes?

A. We all need grace and patience with each other—old to young and young to old. None of us has arrived—not boomers, not Gen X, not millennials. We are to follow our mentors as they follow Christ. They are trying to become more like Jesus. We need to remove the burden of being perfect before we begin to teach others. We just need to be a step ahead. Not perfect.

I define discipleship as "frequently following someone who is spiritually a step ahead of you." I say "frequently" because it is about making this a life. It's not as simple as following a curriculum or memorizing a book.

When I ask, "Do you feel qualified to disciple someone?" people usually will say no. But if I say, "Do you have someone younger you feel like you're spiritually a step ahead of?" the answer almost always is yes.

That means we're ready to follow Christ, even if we stumble. The simple beauty of that Gospel looks very attractive to a generation that has seen the portrayal of "perfect" Christianity break down. Older generations can say, "God's perfect, but He still loves me even when I fall over and over. You'll fall too, but I'm going to try to help you fall less than I did." One of the greatest gifts you can give is letting other people learn from your mistakes.

Q. Ten years from now, what would you dream for the church?

A. That we measure and normalize discipleship in the church. I want it not to be odd. I hope that we wouldn't be wowed by people doing discipleship. Instead, I hope that it's literally what they expect of Christian leaders.

   I don't have the market cornered on this conversation. I'm not saying I have found the way to do it. I'm listening. I've spent a lot of time in serious thought and in prayer and looking at the work, and I found a way that has been effective. (I discuss this in more detail in the book.)

Q. What's our first step in normalizing discipleship?

A. Well, at a church level, measuring. Our models really won't change until we understand where we are.

   Tied to that is simply being clear about what discipleship is and the part it plays in our churches. You'll know you've hit a milestone when you've been so clear about what discipleship is and why it's important that you can get a 100 people in your church to go into 100 separate rooms and give the same answer to the question, "What is our discipleship strategy at this church?" It doesn't have to be a completely common language, but we must have a common goal.

We have to consider that we may have asked people to do something without really giving them any idea what it looks like.

I struggle with the fact that no business would ever get away with how careless the church is about this central mission. Tesla knows exactly how many cars they sold. Chick-fil-A knows exactly how many sandwiches go out the door each day. But go to a church and ask about their disciple-making …

And it's central! We weren't called to start small groups or even to plant churches. Both of those things will happen—if disciples are made.

A church of strong disciple-makers is resilient too. It's not, when built around a single person. That habit isn't healthy and will catch up with us. It's not a healthy situation if a church lives or dies because of one person.

But unfortunately, you don't usually get invited to conferences for being a great discipler. It's about being a great communicator or whatever. When younger people come to me asking for my input, it's usually about being a better speaker. Why? Because that gets more points in the church.

Q. So, looking ahead?

A. I want to encourage people. I'm not trying to make anyone mad. It's very hard to read the Bible and see story after story of discipleship, and then so often the church acts like it's not in there. I mean, we're losing a lot of the next generation. They don't care about a newer or better church marketing event. That was never the game plan. Jesus focused on the 12, not the 5,000. For a long time, I felt like in order to be a great Christian leader you had to be a great speaker, leading your own church.

I once had a mentor tell me, "What you count and what you celebrate creates your culture." We celebrate the gift of speaking more than the gift of pouring into generation after generation.

As the years keep passing, we should actually stop talking so much about millennials and start talking about Gen Z. The concern we should have with millennials is not just how to reach them, but how to train them, how to leverage them, how to send them into action. Millennials are going to have to disciple the next generation in what may be one of the most difficult spiritual climates in history.

Q. Talk for a moment about the unique gifts of millennials to rise to that challenge—we are the great disruptors after all.

A. Yes! Fresh energy. Excitement. We thrive in the challenge of the new and unfamiliar. We adapt fast and are used to traveling lightly in a much more difficult environment than our parents ever had to navigate here in America. There's a reason why church plants attract young people. We are about mission and change, something new and fresh. But it's not just novelty—we also long to be part of something big, where we have responsibility. That fresh perspective and energy can be poured into new things—but it can also restore and revive old ones.

Established churches can be revitalized with some of this new blood, new energy, and new perspective. When young people go all-in with established churches, it's a really beautiful thing. To see that marries the best of both worlds—the resources of older Christians with the passion of the young.

Q. As we wrap up, what fresh idea is on your mind as you continue to encourage the church?

A. There's a verse that's been encouraging me recently—for boomers, millennials, or any Christian as they train the rising generation. It's where Jesus says that His disciples will do "greater things" than He has. Why is there generational tension or indifference? Often, I believe it's because older generations are insecure. They're afraid that this verse is true. I'm not sure many of us really do want the next generation to do greater things than we did. They might do things in a different way. They might mess up what we did. That can be scary.

But we need to sincerely want the success of those younger than we are. I once was speaking on a panel at a large event. They sat me next to a 19-year-old kid—about a decade younger than I am. He has been doing these evangelistic crusades globally. Just out of high school! This kid was talking about the "next generation," and I'm thinking, Wow. He's doing way more than I did at that age. And even I have to say, "Do I make this about me, or do I want to help that guy get farther faster than I could ever have gone?"

I once heard David Platt say something to this effect—that we all want to raise Jesus' name. The problem is that many of us internally want our name to rise with his.

Think of Jesus—He sincerely wanted His followers to do greater things than He did. Or think of David. Saul gave one of the biggest responsibilities ever to this young guy. David didn't seem qualified or equipped to fight a giant. He literally wasn't even in the military, from what we understand. But Saul allowed him to face the giant. I think that's one of the biggest things that Saul ever did. No one gives him credit for it. He gambled everything on the next generation, and it worked, and it was massive. If only he'd been OK with David's success.

Israel won because of what this guy did, and it only went bad after Saul saw his reputation pale next to David's name. Do boomers and Gen Xers want millennials to do greater things for the Kingdom than they did? Or are they trying to hang on to the credit? That's not going to work. We know Christ is going to get it all in the end.

We're on the same team. All of us.

## Notable Quotes from Above

This generation is dying to be a part of something bigger than they are. Unfortunately, the world sometimes gives young adults bigger responsibilities than the church does.

The church has lost the message of "Come, follow me," replacing it with ... what? 'Come and listen to me'?

My generation needs to show up more, I think—and be willing to stay when things get tough.

There's such a culture in the church of making fun of the next generation. Dismissing them, demeaning them. Why are we shocked that young people don't want to go to churches that have that kind of culture?

If you're really saying to someone, "Come, follow me," then you're not adding another event to your calendar. You're including someone in your calendar. That's discipleship.

This generation has been marketed at by older people their whole lives. They are really good at sniffing out when someone isn't genuine.

Our job isn't to be relevant; our job is to make disciples. Those disciples will be more "relevant" than we could ever be.

Millennials are going to have to disciple the next generation in what may be one of the most difficult spiritual climates in history.

## Facts

1. Though 7 in 10 young people leave the church once entering college, as many as two-thirds of them will return later. —LifeWay Research

2. Today, half of American pastors are older than 55. In 1992, 24% were that old. Pastors 65 and older have almost tripled in the last 25 years, from 6% to 17%. Meanwhile, pastors 40 and younger have fallen from 33% in 1992 to 15% today. —LifeWay Research

3. Research shows 60% of millennials donate an average of $481 to nonprofits every year. It's not that millennials aren't givers; they just don't share the default opinion of prior generations that giving charitable money to the church is the best way for donations to be distributed. —Pushpay

---

**iWork4Him Show**

- http://bit.ly/2Lw0RKo

---

---

[1] **Paul J. Pastor** is editor-at-large of Outreach, an editor of books, and author of multiple titles including *The Face of the Deep*, *The Listening Day*, and *Palau: A Life on Fire* (with Luis Palau). He lives in Oregon.

# Part III

## *Resources to Activate Your Faith in Retirement*

To start your new journey in retirement through the iRetire4Him lens, you're going to need some resources designed to equip you. It's time to get out of the grandstands of life and onto the playing field.

These resources are designed to help you hear from God and shape your retirement years. Enjoy the journey.

Remember to visit www.iRetire4Him.com for updated resources and recordings.

# 17

## iRetire4Him Recommended Books and Website Resources

### Books on Retirement

1. *The Retirement Reformation* – Bruce Bruinsma

2. *Charting Your Course: Planning for Your Next Three Decades* – Bruce Bruinsma

3. *An Uncommon Guide to Retirement: Finding God's Purpose for the Next Season of Life* – Jeff Haanen

4. *The Retirement Revolution* – David Kennon

5. *Halftime & Finishing Well* – Bob Buford

6. *Rethinking Retirement: Finishing Life for the Glory of Christ* – John Piper

7. *Launch your ENCORE: Finding Adventure and Purpose Later in Life* – Finzel/Hicks

8. *The New Retirementality* – Mitch Anthony

9. *Third Calling: What are you doing the rest of your life?* – Dr. Richard and Leona Bergstrom

## Books to Understand the Generations

1. *Millennials Matter* – Danita Bye

2. *The Passion Generation* – Grant Skeldon

3. *Sticking Points: How to Get 4 Generations Working Together in the 12 Places They Come Apart* – Haydn Shaw

4. *Generational IQ: Christianity Isn't Dying, Millennials Aren't the Problem, and the Future Is Bright* – Haydn Shaw

## Website Resources Focused on Discipling and Utilizing Retirees.

1. www.RetirementReformation.org
2. www.Halftime.org
3. www.c12group.com
4. www.MarketplaceChaplains.org
5. www.CorporateChaplains.org
6. www.PTL.org

# 18

---

# 14 Stories of Faith
# in Retirement

---

*Stories From the iWork4Him Talk Show*

## 1. Ross Harrop

Newly retired Boy Scouts executive Ross Harrop shares his journey to becoming a C12 chair.

- http://bit.ly/2Kwr5MI

## 2. Wally Armstrong

Great words from our phenomenal guest and retired PGA Tour Pro, Wally Armstrong, joined Jim, along with local CBMC Chair, Mark Graham, for a chat on ministry on the golf course. It was a great hour filled with laughs, testimony, heartfelt conversation, and some pretty nifty golf tips.

- http://bit.ly/3q3BVsn

## 3. Diane Paddison

Martha interviews newly retired executive and author Diane Paddison, whose book and women-centered workplace ministry, 4word women, focus on the principle of placing a priority on workplace relationships while also honoring God.

- http://bit.ly/3opxN5V

## 4. Auntie Anne Beiler

Her glory is her story, so says Auntie Anne Beiler of the famed—and delicious—Auntie Anne Pretzels, and she broke down more of her Glory Story with us on today's program. It's a remarkably relatable testimony filled with savory nuggets you can sink your teeth into as she has moved from corporate CEO to a "retired" speaker.

- http://bit.ly/2Xje8bA

## 5. Ward Brehm

What happens when the Lord gives you the world and all your dreams and wishes by the age of 40? We found out exactly that with Ward Brehm and his brand-new book, *Bigger Than Me*. Ward got super transparent in our conversation about how success left him empty inside and how our Lord laid on his heart a mission that would impact a continent! Hear from Ward Brehm as he shares his perspective from a newly minted retirement.

- http://bit.ly/2LfPLsZ

## 6. Bill Wolf

We were honored to chat with newly re-fired Bill Wolf as he comes out of retirement and his longtime co-worker Roger Ross. They talked about their new company, Think Utility Services, about their faith stories, how they bring Jesus into their workspace, and how they impact every day by combining their faith and work.

- http://bit.ly/2MBckIY

## 7. Bruce Bruinsma

We got a rethinking of retirement today with Bruce Bruinsma of the ministry, "Retirement Reformation," to get a glimpse of what it means to retire4Him. It was an eye-popping conversation that will shift your financial thinking in the best way possible.

- http://bit.ly/39b1n8K

## 8. David Kennon

Better yet, how about we discuss a retirement *revolution*! How should we be saving—and spending—our retirement dollars as we go into the sunset. Is there a right and wrong way? A biblical way? These are the topics you'll learn about as Jim and Martha bring on author Dave Kennon to break down his book, *The Retirement Revolution*, and blow your mind.

- http://bit.ly/3hQSmpl

## 9. Bob Spence

Great pinch-hitting guest host this week saw Pastor Couch talk faith and work with newly retired Convene chairman Bob Spence.

- http://bit.ly/2LAakAs

## 10. Dave Zillig

Dave Zillig talks about how to work out your faith in a workplace filled with millennials. He also spoke about how he, as a retiree, is investing his wisdom and experience in the next generation.

- http://bit.ly/38occFe

## 11. Mark Dillon

Newly retired Mark Dillon talks about being intentional for Christ in the workplace.

- http://bit.ly/3hTF7nH

## 12. Martin Newby

On the program today are Martin Newby and Peter Swanson of LoveServes International. The purpose of Love-Serves is to bring the love of Christ to the people of the Dominican Republic. A truly inspiring story of humble beginnings resulting in the service of needs for believers in the region, this message is of hope and humanity.

- http://bit.ly/2XkHB59

## 13. Doug Piper

Jim has highlighted the book *Halftime* during segments and shows before, but today's program spotlights the life-changing effect it had on Doug Piper. Doug's retirement paradigm completely shifted after being introduced to *Halftime*, but not before doing a bit of intensive research of his own.

- http://bit.ly/35kcfzM

## 14. Ken Snodgrass

Author, Ken Snodgrass, talks about his groundbreaking work, *Trading with God: Seven Steps to Integrate Your Faith into Your Work*, which addresses the Christian faith's relevancy in today's workplace. We get in-depth about each one of these integral steps in this podcast as we talk with this retiree.

- http://bit.ly/3hTOdkz

# 19

## The iWork4Him Trilogy

*IRETIRE4HIM: UNLOCK GOD'S Purpose for Your Retirement* is part of a trilogy that God has put together. The other two titles are *iWork4Him: Change the Way You Think About Your Faith at Work* and *sheWorks4Him: Embrace Your Calling as a Christian Woman at Work*. The following two chapters are the introductions to *iWork4Him* and *sheWorks4Him*. These books are a collaborative effort with dozens of contributors specifically focused on giving practical, tactical, factual, and biblical perspectives to the Christian working women, everyday believers, and the retiree. You will find each of these books has a unique perspective that will continue your journey or help someone you know grow where they are. All three books are available at www.iWork4Him.com/bookstore.

### *iWork4Him* Introduction

A successful hike into the deep woods requires some useful tools. A seasoned hiker might suggest a compass, a GPS, or specific gear based on the terrain. Veterans even publish booklets to instruct and ensure a better journey.

Any way you look at it, you need something to keep you on the right path and headed in the right direction.

Believers need tools and resources for our workplace mission field. We need a guide providing information and how-to's to live out our faith journey in our work. *iWork4Him* is dedicated to that effort.

iWork4Him is a statement of faith. It's a lifestyle that impacts everything we do. It is a permanent paradigm shift in our minds. Being able to say "iWork4Him" demonstrates a deepening of our faith. It is Jesus coming alive in us, in our work.

> Don't copy the behavior and customs of this world, but let God transform you into a new person by changing the way you think. Then you will learn to know God's will for you, which is good and pleasing and perfect.
> (Rom. 12:2 NLT)

So how do we live the iWork4Him lifestyle? How do we stop compartmentalizing our faith while doing our work? How do we apply Romans 12:2 and stop copying the world? We first go to the Bible as our primary resource because it is filled with God's wisdom and examples for living out our faith. We wrote *iWork4Him* as a secondary resource providing the practical, tactical, factual, and biblical resources on how you can live out your faith in your work.

For years, iWork4Him has had a front-row seat to the move of God in the workplaces of Christ-followers in America. We have heard the stories, conducted interviews, and covered the conferences and workshops that focus on this topic. We have gathered these stories and resources in this book to guide us on the path to saying iWork4Him.

You are called to work. It is a gift from God. He created work as a way for us to partner with Him. The workplace is the largest ministry opportunity in the world, and God wants you to join Him there. Let's get ready to go in the field—the mission field of your work. May this journey be life-changing. Permanently.

## *sheWorks4Him* Introduction

I am so excited for you to read *sheWorks4Him: Embrace Your Calling as a Christian Woman at Work*. Each chapter has been written by a Christian working woman who has been our guest on *The iWork4Him show*. We have heard their hearts on the air and asked them to share their unique work experiences in this book. Each chapter also includes thought-provoking, spiritually challenging questions designed to help you shape your perspective as a Christian working woman. These can work in a small group of trusted friends or just with you and the Lord all alone.

Why did we do this project? Because as a Christian working woman, you need to know you are not the only one struggling to live out your purpose in your work. We learn a lot from other people's faith stories, so it is our hope and prayer that each chapter helps you feel more celebrated, validated, understood, and resourced for living out your faith in your work.

I have never met a woman who wasn't working hard, trying to be everything to everyone. Your workplace may be at home or in a high-rise; almost all women suffer from trying to do it all. TJ Tison describes this complex in her book, *Killing Wonder Women* (TJ wrote a chapter in *iWork4Him: Change the Way You Think About Your Faith at Work*). We want you to embrace who God created you to be, not fulfill the expectations of culture or the church.

God has given you a unique set of gifts, talents, and abilities. Your spiritual gifts are from Him. First Peter 4:10 NLT says, "God has given each of you a gift from his great variety of spiritual gifts. Use them well to serve one another." He gifted you to do the things you are doing. He placed you in the workplace you are in because He needed and wanted you there. You were called into the world to be a living and breathing example of the Gospel in your work. As you turn each page, you will see how God has led these Christian working women to serve in their job more effectively, using their unique giftedness.

Sisters, you are a gift and a blessing. With your busy schedule, it's easy to let your priorities suffer. Remember this. Your number one priority is growing in your life with Christ, getting closer to the Father every day. All other priorities seem to fall in order when we keep Him as our number one.

The amazing women who wrote each chapter are willingly sharing a part of their story to both encourage and challenge you. I pray that it will launch you with renewed purpose in your workplace mission field.

—**Jim Brangenberg,** Talk Show Host and Mentor,
   www.iWork4Him.com

# 20

## Commit Your Life to Jesus: First Time or Recommitment

DEAR FRIENDS,

By the age of 57, I had lived a good life, ignored my Catholic roots, and allowed God to be an afterthought. A friend invited me to church, and I thought it wouldn't hurt to learn more about God. The pastor explained the Bible in a relatable way, and before long, I was learning to love others because I realized that Jesus loved me unconditionally. There's more to the story, but I took that first step, and now I have a personal relationship with Jesus.

**— The fellow Retiree from the Dedication Page – Gary (Jim's Brother-in-Law)**

I became a follower of Jesus at 13, while my youth pastor was mentoring me. I made this decision after seeing that life on my own was headed towards a dead end. Jesus said in John 10:10, "The thief's purpose is to steal and kill and destroy. My purpose is to give them a rich and satisfying life" (NLT). I had seen the thief's work in my life. It left me empty and hopeless. Jesus's plan for my life was the answer I was looking for. I think you will see why.

**—Jim**

*The following pages by the Pocket Testament League will help you understand God's ultimate rescue plan for you. This is what changed my life.*

*If you would like a copy of the Gospel of John, send an email to Jim@iWork4Him.com.*

## A True Story in Your Hands

The Bible is an eyewitness account of history that has stood the test of time and made a difference to billions of lives around the world.

- Have you ever wondered why you are here on earth?

- Have you ever had a sense that you were made for more?

- Have you ever been amazed by the beauty of this world? Or the wonder of love? While at the same time also being shocked and discouraged by the hatred and evil around us?

## There's a Reason You Feel This Way ... You Were Designed for Good

God created the world, and that includes you—and He declared everything He made to be good! In fact, He says you're "very good" because you come from Him!

That longing you have inside yourself for the world to "be right" may seem like an echo—here one moment and gone the next—but don't be confused, that sense of longing comes from God.

Not only do you come from God, but you have purpose. The Bible says that your purpose is to be with God in a world of love and beauty and meaning.

We know that something is wrong—and it is us. It's me and you.

Without God, we choose to live for ourselves. You might think of it as walking away from God.

The Bible calls that SIN. Take a moment and ask yourself, "Do I do things I know are wrong?"

If we are honest with ourselves, we will admit we rebel … we sin.

When we sin, we break our relationship with God. And everything that was meant for our good gets broken.

## Can We Fix This Problem?

Great question! We cannot. Many have tried. Many try to build a bridge to God.

Have you ever tried? Tried to live perfectly? It's impossible, right?

The problem is BIGGER than you may realize. Sin separates us from God forever.

## But God Intervened Because He Loves You!

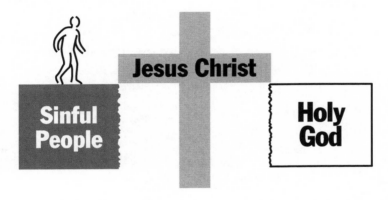

> For God so loved the world that He gave his one and only Son, that whoever believes in Him shall not perish but have eternal life. (John 3:16 NIV)

What you can't do through your own efforts, God the Son, Jesus, did by coming to earth to die on the cross for you. He took the punishment for your sin. Jesus became the way between God the Father and you. Jesus Christ is the only way for us to reach the Father (John 14:6).

## What Does All That Mean?

- It means that you can have a real, meaningful life—today and forever. "I have come that they may have life, and have it to the full" (John 10:10 NIV).

- It means that when you believe in Jesus, you are restored to the "very good" relationship you were created for... you become God's son or daughter. "Yet to all who did receive him, to those who believed in his name, he gave the right to become children of God" (John 1:12 NIV).

- It means that you can live with passion and purpose because you walk in a loving relationship with the One who created you, serving Him and sharing the Good News of His love with others—reconciling the world to God.

## How Can I Know God?

There are three steps to take:

1. Admit that you need God and turn away from sin (see John 8:11).

2. Believe (have faith) that when Jesus died on the cross, He took the punishment for all your sin, and He rose to life again to conquer death (see John 1:29).

3. Receive (ask) Jesus Christ as your Lord and Savior.

## A Simple Prayer

Here is a prayer to receive Jesus Christ as your Lord and Savior. It is a suggested prayer. The exact wording doesn't matter, what counts is the attitude of your heart:

> Lord Jesus, thank You for showing me how much I need You. Thank You for dying on the cross for me. I believe that You are who You say You are and that You rose from the dead to conquer sin and death. Please forgive all my failures and sins. Make me clean and help me start fresh with You. I now receive You into my life as my Lord and Savior. Help me to love and serve You with all my heart. Amen.

Jesus said: "Whoever comes to me I will never drive away" (John 6:37 NIV).

## What's Next? It Depends

If you prayed the prayer, congratulations. Becoming a follower of Jesus is only the beginning of an exciting adventure. You are invited to read this entire Gospel of John, turn to the back of this booklet, and sign that you've responded to Jesus's call. We've included some additional pages with what to do next and links about where to find resources for the journey ahead.

If you are not ready to respond to Jesus's call, consider reading about Jesus. When people would meet Jesus and ask him questions, his answer was, "Come and see."

So, come and see. You're invited to meet Jesus.

Read the Book of John (if you don't have a Bible, email me for a book of John: jim@iWork4him.com)

The Book of John is an eyewitness account of the life, death, and resurrection of Jesus of Nazareth. John wrote this account with a special theme in mind that he states near the end:

> But these are written that you may believe that Jesus is the Messiah, the Son of God, and that by believing you may have life in his name. (John 20:31 NIV)

## My Response

If God has spoken to you and you are ready to follow Jesus, fill out this page as a reminder of your response.

I hear God calling me, and I now know that my sin separates me from Him. Because God loves me, He sent His Son, Jesus Christ, to pay the penalty for my sin by dying on the cross to restore me to fellowship with God. I have asked Jesus to forgive my sins and give me eternal life. It is my desire to love Him and obey His Word.

Name _____

Date of Response _____

*Visit www.ptl.org/response and let us know about your life-changing response. We'll send you information about free resources you can use to grow closer to God.*

## Follow Me

Jesus loves people, and people are curious about Jesus. Jesus's solution is simple. Follow me. For centuries, people have been doing just that: following Jesus.

Becoming a follower of Jesus is only the beginning of an exciting journey. Jesus called it being "born again" (see John 3:3). It means that you now have a personal relationship with God as your heavenly Father. You are not alone. God sent the Holy Spirit from heaven to be your Counselor, to guide you into all truth (see John 14:26; 15:26; and 16:12–15). He will help you live each day for God and to accept the changes He wants to make in your life. You can depend on His power to enable you to grow as a follower of Jesus.

Being a follower of Jesus involves a whole new life. Start now:

- ✓ *Read* a part of the Bible each day.
- ✓ *Pray* daily; talk to God as you would to a close friend.
- ✓ *Worship* God by attending a church where the Bible is taught.
- ✓ *Join* with other followers for support and encouragement.
- ✓ *Share* your faith in Christ by offering people one of these Gospels.

*Want to learn more?* For a free course on the Gospel of John or to join The Pocket Testament League as a Member (membership is free), visit www.ptl.org/follow.

## About the League

The Pocket Testament League is an interdenominational evangelical organization founded in 1893 when a teenage girl and her friends made a commitment to carry pocket-sized New Testaments to share with others. The League encourages followers of Jesus everywhere to Read, Carry and Share God's Word. Learn more about The Pocket Testament League by visiting www.ptl.org/about.

## Statement of Faith

The Pocket Testament League adheres to the following statement of faith:

- ✝ The inspiration and authority of the whole Bible (Old and New Testaments) as the full revelation of God by the Holy Spirit.
- ✝ The Deity of the Lord Jesus Christ, His virgin birth, His substitutionary atoning death on the cross, His bodily resurrection, and His personal return.
- ✝ The necessity of the new birth for entering the Kingdom of God, as described in John 3.
- ✝ The obligation upon all believers to be witnesses of the Lord Jesus Christ and to seek the salvation of others.

## Reach the World for Christ! Join the Movement.

If God has spoken to you through His Word, join us today. Go to www.ptl.org/join and click on JOIN NOW. If there is a number in the box below, enter it in the Referral ID field *when you sign up*.

*Take the 21-day challenge*. Read through the Gospel of John and grow closer to God. Track your progress with your personal dashboard and earn points as you Read, Carry and Share God's Word in the form of pocket-sized testaments. Visit www.ptl.org/marathon to get started!

THE POCKET TESTAMENT LEAGUE®
PO Box 800
Lititz, PA 17543
www.ptl.org

# More from iWork4Him

# For the working woman
# in your life

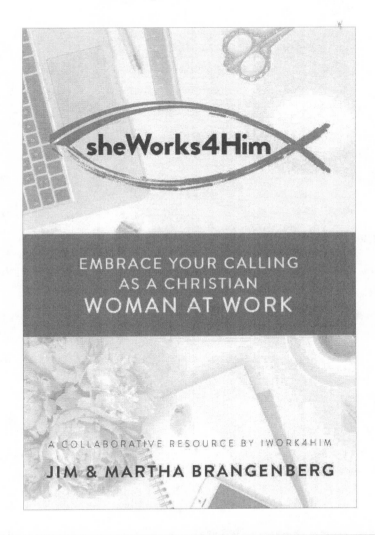